STRICTLY OFF THE RECORD

GRAND PRIX CONTROVERSY AND INTRIGUE

The line-out plus a potentially competitive car, and the wish came true. With Tim Parnell, Alex Stokes, Aubrey Woods, Jackie Oliver, and Pedro Rodriguez.

LOUIS T. STANLEY

STRICTLY OFF THE RECORD

GRAND PRIX CONTROVERSY AND INTRIGUE

BRMs in Yardley livery, an enjoyable and successful sponsorship for both parties

MBI Publishing Company

DEDICATED TO MY WIFE JEAN

This edition first published in 1999 by MBI Publishing Company,
729 Prospect Avenue, PO Box 1, Osceola, WI 54020-0001 USA

MBI Publishing Company books are also available at discounts in bulk quantity for industrial or sales-
promotional use. For details write to Special Sales Manager at Motorbooks International Wholesalers &
Distributors, 729 Prospect Avenue, PO Box 1, Osceola, WI 54020-0001 USA.

Library of Congress Cataloging-in-Publication Data Available

ISBN 0-7603-0737-7

CREDITS

Editor: Richard O'Neill
Designers: John Heritage, Mark Holt
Filmset: SX Composing Limited, England
Mono reproduction: P&W Graphics, Singapore
Printed in Italy

THE AUTHOR

Louis Stanley is one of the most controversial and best known figures in motor racing. The editor
of *Veteran and Vintage* once wrote "Sponsors come and go. So do world champions and the cars
they drive, but Louis Stanley goes marching on, controversial, candid and merciless. Like another
veteran in a field totally divorced from the automobile - he does it his way," to which *The Times*
correspondent added "Louis Stanley's stripping of the grand prix scene creates (among those who
dare admit it) more tremors than a Cape Kennedy blast-off." In *Strictly Off the Record* Louis
Stanley repeats the treatment.

ACKNOWLEDGEMENTS

All photographs by Louis Stanley except Niki Lauda, page 6, courtesy of Getty Images.

Contents

Foreword
by Niki Lauda

It was with immense pleasure that I agreed to write the Foreword to *Strictly Off the Record*. Its author, Louis Stanley gave me enormous encouragement at the start of my racing career. We first met on Christmas Eve at Vienna airport to discuss the terms of my contract with BRM. We broke off so I could discuss the deal with my parents and lawyers while Louis went to St. Stephen's Cathedral to hear the Vienna Boys' Choir sing the traditional Christmas Eve carol service. I signed the contract before Louis' plane left for London. With team-mates Jean-Pierre Beltoise and Clay Regazzoni I gained invaluable experience at BRM before moving on to Ferrari.

Louis Stanley is a remarkable man by any standards. Some time ago fellow driver Jackie Stewart wrote an appreciation of Louis' contribution to the sport of motor racing and I share the sentiment that is expressed in the following extract:

Left: Three-times World Champion Niki Lauda in 1975, a year before his near-fatal crash.

> *"Louis Stanley wears many hats in motor racing, and has coats of many colours. He is a man of strong convictions. He undertakes many tasks, some of which seem impossible. He executes these with no concern for his personal popularity because, in some instances, he is driving directly against convention and sometimes The Establishment as we in motor racing know it. The duties he undertakes would fill the lifetime of lesser men. In all his dealings and efforts his beliefs are sincere. His interest in racing is intense, and to many drivers his presence is assuring and comforting when things are not well. In cases of accidents he has been a pillar of strength to the people most clearly affected by this side of motor racing."*

This was abundantly clear when I crashed on the first lap of the German Grand Prix at the Nürburgring. My car was engulfed in flames and my injuries were so serious that medics thought I would die. I was saved due to the specialised treatment I received at the hands of Europe's finest burns specialist, flown in by Louis. It was just another example of his spontaneous, selfless reaction to a crisis.

Strictly Off the Record offers reminders of the years when motor-racing was an adventure and of the long list of drivers, many of whom were close personal friends, who were killed on the track. There are reminders too of the lighter moments, and of the personalities surrounding the sport from the early years right up to the motor-racing scene of today.

NIKI LAUDA

1
No Turning Back the Clock!

I nevitably *Strictly Off the Record* reflects bias and personal reminiscences gar-
nered from some fifty years of motor-racing involvement. Maybe the tone is
more tolerant than it used to be. I put that down to having to accept reluctantly that the sport has changed beyond recall. Indulging in unashamed nostalgia by recalling the years when it was a genuine sport though by no means perfect. Some flaws persist like political
wrangling, intrigues and rule-bending
with constant reminders that it was
potentially lethal. So many friends
were killed. Attempts to make circuits
safer and improve medical facilities
were opposed by a hard core of officials and jaundiced journalists who
wanted a gladiatorial sport provided
their skins were safe.

Camaraderie among entrants
and drivers is a thing of the past, likewise a sense of caring. Greed is the
motivation. All levels are affected.
Purists know it can never be the same
and take comfort that memories never
age. If only it were possible to have a
Mori Poll reaction from the racing public, but that is wishful thinking.

Instead I turn the spotlight on
the activities of a man who single-
handed has contrived the destruction
of the old order and in the process has
established himself as dictator of the
sport. That man is Bernie Ecclestone.
In doing so I am conscious that too
close a personal acquaintance can be a
deterrent. He is a remarkable man,
small in stature, just over 5 feet, but compensated by marrying a strikingly beau-
tiful girl who must be 6 feet. Like many successful people, Bernie's background
was frugal and cash-strapped. His father, a trawler captain, pandered to the lad's
interest in mechanics, let him work in a motor-cycle shop, and try his hand at
motor-cycle racing on dirt tracks, then progressing to cars, graduating to Formula
One racing as an observer. He became commercial manager to Jochen Rindt and

I recall vividly walking down the long corridor of a Milan hospital after the World Champion had died from injuries with the sad task of breaking the news to his wife Nina who was waiting with Colin Chapman and Bernie Ecclestone, whose quiet sympathy was an enormous help. Like then, he seems to be ever-present whenever a crisis occurs. The persistence has paid off. He was not intimidated by the fact that the sport was dominated by rich, egotistical amateurs, a club for gentlemen with the right background and a taste for speed and glamour. They just wanted to race. Entrants and engineers were not interested in the business side and welcomed Ecclestone's offer to negotiate deals with circuit owners and handle team travel arrangements for a fee. That became the strategy and it paid off. Becoming owner of the Brabham Formula One team; in 1972 thereby qualifying to attend his first meeting of the F.I. Constructor's Association. From then on there was no looking back. In 1981 the FIA empowered him to negotiate television deals, later inviting him to become Vice-President. The key to his ambitions was packaging motor-racing into a spectacular, colourful presentation that would encourage sponsorship. December 13th, 1995 saw this happen. Ecclestone had a

Left: Baron Huschke von Hanstein, Prince Paul von Mitterind and Louis Stanley - figures of the old regime

meeting with Jonathan Martin, head of BBC Sport, and told him he intended to sell the United Kingdom rights to broadcast Formula One to ITV. The deal could be off if the BBC improved on a figure of £65 million. Such a payment was impossible. Grand Prix racing has since benefited by an income that totals millions of pounds. Viewing audiences are 300 million for each race. He has made deals for live TV transmission on a global scale and attracted multi-million sponsorship deals with international companies.

Ecclestone has now established himself as supreme boss of every Formula One commercial activity. Rule changes are made if by so doing television viewing is made more exciting. He decides which countries qualify for a Grand Prix. He has turned Formula One racing into a billion-pound business. At the same time his personal fortune is estimated at some £1.5 billion. Not bad for the skint son of a trawler skipper.

One aspect of Ecclestone's dealings is an unfortunate reluctance to reveal facts about his web of companies. He does not court publicity, possibly because there has been no need to disclose his involvements. He is entitled to take such a line, but openness is far preferable. The racing public would be interested to know if the Ecclestone portfolio of companies includes one that promotes many of the races; a hospitality company, a travel company; a digital television company; an engine company; sponsorship-broking company, film production company plus one final query. Is it true that there is a twenty-five year agreement between the Formula One Group and the FIA, if so, what are the details? It would be a courtesy to the racing public if these and other points were clarified.

Shrewd and calculating, Ecclestone is not always right. His plans for the flotation of his Formula One Group were jolted by the decision of the European

Below: Oliver Bertram, barrister by profession, remembered for his handling of the 10 litre Delage and the 8 litre Bentley which he lapped at 142 mph.

Centre: Lord Essendon as the Hon. Brian Lewis, one of the leading British drivers in the post-war years.

Below: Earl Howe, former President of the BRDC.

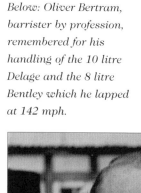

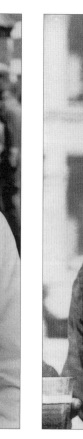

Competition Commissioner to hold an investigation into his sports business dealings. Karel Van Miert is concerned about the power Ecclestone wields. There are in fact two investigations. One involving the FIA and the second completely separate investigation into Ecclestone's competitive practices with his FOA. In the meantime, flotation plans have been put on ice. In its place is a decision to take out a £1.2 billion Euro bond issue into a trust ensuring the continuing wealth of his wife and children. Morgan Stanley Dean Witter, the investment bank, staged a presentation to 200 investors at London's Grosvenor House Hotel. Karl Essig, a Morgan Stanley director, went through the details of the bond to the potential investors. There seemed to be unease about the complexities of the Formula One business and talk about the possible effect of the European Commission investigation. Various legal manoeuvres were mooted, but the consensus was to wait for the EC ruling. Bernie is adept at handling motor-racing projects, but coping with the City and its politics is a different ball game. One advantage of a Eurobond issue is that it does not require answers to awkward areas that a flotation prospectus might be obliged to probe.

In the meantime a belt-and-braces alternative has surfaced. A consortium believed to include HSBC bank and venture capital groups Apax and Mezzanine Management may revive a £2-billion plan to buy Formula One from Ecclestone, who would receive shares as well as a lump sum. One of the principals involved is Samengo-Turner who fronted a team competing in the World Championship so knows the ropes at first-hand.

To end on a happier note, Bernie has the satisfaction of knowing he has successfully commercialised every aspect of the sport. It thrives though perhaps not as purists would like, but then, you can't please everyone.

Centre: Baron de Graffenreid, effervescent and candid.

Below: Count de Villapaderna played a prominent role in restoring Spain to the World Championship rota. Tall and aristocratic, sophisticated and oracular, he outshone many of his continental colleagues.

Below: Maurice Baumgartner, conservative-minded President of the CSI.

2
Men Who Enriched the Sport

COLIN CHAPMAN

Colin Chapman was one of the most significant figures in Grand Prix racing, certainly the most mentally agile. His achievements put him in a class of his own. It began in 1953. Colin, a talented but impecunious engineering student of London University and de Havilland apprenticed, decided to branch out on his own. His fiancée, Hazel Williams, approved and put £25 in the kitty. His first Lotus 'factory', a stable in Tottenham Lane, Hornsey, was formally registered as the Lotus Engineering Company; its product, a tubular space frame chassis with stressed aluminium panels; asking price £100. There was no shortage of customers.

From such modest beginnings grew the Lotus Group of Companies with ultra-modern factories, test-track facilities, runways for aircraft, boat-building plant and Ketteringham Hall, an impressive country home and estate. Of the many projects, Colin concentrated on Team Lotus with its separate financial existence alongside the publicly-quoted Lotus Group. Colin's obsession was justified with 72 World Championship Grand Prix victories, five World Championships, six World Constructors Championships and an Indianapolis '500' win. Enough to satisfy most mortals, but not Colin.

Mentally and physically restless, he kept experimenting with innovations. His robust constitution was tested to the limit. Eventually the strain took its toll. After a meeting in Paris of the Formula One Commission, he flew home to Norwich that evening. In the early hours of the morning, a massive heart attack proved fatal. The responsibility of designing cars, running the Formula One racing team, managing the Companies in a competitive market and the controversial De Lorean deal proved too much. At 54 years he was burnt out with overwork. Maybe delegation might have helped but that was not Colin's way. He was a one-man legend.

In a montage of recollections, I think of Colin's first cigar-shaped, front-engined machine that made its début in the 1958 French Grand Prix; of innumerable experiments, like the monocoque chassis, stressed engines and inboard front brakes; the break-through that produced the four-wheel-drive and turbined-engined racing car that would have won the Indy '500' had a bearing not failed; his excitement at the results of the Types 78 and 79 ground-effect cars that gave Lotus temporary technical superiority; the revolutionary twin-chassis Lotus 88 that took advantage of the downforce generated under the bodywork. These are but some of the 91 designs created by Colin's analytical calculations.

One area was not pursued. Unlike Ferrari and BRM, Colin did not build his own engines. Instead he relied on Coventry-Climax before switching to the Ford-financed Cosworth V8 in 1967 and establishing a meaningful working relation-

Right: Colin concentrating on lap-times. Hazel, calm, unflappable, waiting to take over.

ship with Walter Hayes who did so much to revolutionize the sport behind the scenes. Running parallel, Colin's aerodynamic designed sports cars were renowned for superb road-holding characteristics superior to their commercial rivals. As an aside, I recall the first Lotus Grand Prix win, achieved not by a works entry but in the Type 18 privately entered by Rob Walker and driven by Stirling Moss in Monaco.

On a personal note, my recollections of Colin cover some 30 years. Two in particular were traumatic. I had a telephone call from James Clark in Berwickshire. He told me that his son Jim had been killed in a crash at Hockenheim and asked if I would go to the scene of the accident with their family lawyer. Shortly

afterwards a Lear jet touched down at Cambridge airport and we left for Frankfurt. The cause of the crash was uncertain. It occurred on the curving right-hand sweep on the fastest sector of the track. The circuit was wet and cars were throwing up clouds of spray. According to a marshal, the Lotus swerved to the near side, then to the off, went out of control, left the track sideways, demolished a steel fence post and hit a tree. Further details were released later in an official report. The force of the impact caused the car structure to fail in tension at the rear of the bulkhead, the engine and transmission unit with the rear wheels finishing some 20 yards away. The radiator was torn off. The nose section went into another tree. The steering column broke, steering damper and brake fluid reser-

Left: Colin behind the Lotus that, due to his inspired designing skill, won six Drivers' and seven Constructors' World Campionships.

Left: Keith Duckworth, engineer-designer: innovative, not afraid of experimenting.

voirs were torn away. The tachometer read 7,200 rpm, equivalent to 125 mph on the gearing of the car. The throttle had jammed open due to a combination of maximum throttle cable pull and immense download on the linkage to the fuel metering unit. There was no evidence of pre-structural failure and Jim Clark was in no way to blame. Such details show how structurally today's racing cars have improved. At Hockenheim Armco-barriers would have prevented the Lotus plunging into the forest. Clark might have escaped with minor injuries. The carnage at Spa in the 1990 Belgian Grand Prix demonstrated how drivers can walk away unscathed from major crashes. In the 'sixties, the CSI were reluctant to enforce elementary safety standards. As a result our greatest racing driver was killed.

Right: After Jochen Rindt's death, Chapman almost withdrew from the sport, but was persuaded to continue. He became preoccupied by pressing matters concerning his car company.

The effect of that tragedy on Colin was devastating. He had real empathy with Jim. They spoke the same language, saw eye-to-eye on car preparation and race tactics. On the return journey the coffin was placed in a charter plane at Frankfurt. Seats were removed so that the bier could be secured. Colin was seated alongside. Grief is a very personal moment, but it was heart-rending to witness Colin's distress. There was further tension. The plane took off. Thirty minutes later the pilot's window smashed. All pressure was lost. The plane descended and managed to limp back to Frankfurt where emergency plans had been alerted.

The second memory, also sad, is linked with Jochen Rindt's horrific crash in the Italian Grand Prix at Monza. The moment occurred in the hospital at Milan. I left the operating theatre and walked down the corridor where Colin was waiting with Nina and Bernie Ecclestone. I had to break the news that Jochen was dead. His wife, drained of emotion, was impassive, Colin was in shock. After the Clark tragedy his attitude to racing had become subdued. Rindt's death under-lined the guilt feeling of being involved in a sport that caused meaningless loss of life. The passage of time helps but it was never quite the same, even Emerson Fittipaldi's championship win in a Lotus lacked the old sparkle. The dilemma was one that we all had to face in those days.

A third memory is slightly out of character. It is linked with Churchill College, Cambridge. Colin was invited to dinner by the Master, Sir William Hawthorne, who was also Head of the Engineering Faculty. I sat next to Colin at High Table. Afterwards in the Combination Room we were joined by Professor

Paul Dykes, known in engineering circles as designer of the *Dykes Ring*. I expected the trend of conversation to be technical. Instead Colin showed more interest in aspects of the experimental physics facet of Cavendish Laboratories, particularly the work of the physicist James Clerk Maxwell. Paul Dykes described how Maxwell's main achievements were in the understanding of eletromagnetic waves, his equations bringing together electricity, magnetism and light in one set of relations. By studying gases, optics and the sensation of colour, Maxwell's theoretical work in magnetism prepared the way for wireless telegraphy and telephony. At times it was difficult to follow the full implications, but there was no doubt about Colin's interest, particularly how Maxwell finally proved that heat resides in the motion of molecules. On more mundane matters, Colin asked about the inscription on the base of the marble bust of Maxwell at the entrance to the Cavendish. It was dp/dt. Dykes explained that this differential coefficient was Maxwell's favourite pun on his initials. In the second law of thermodynamics dp/dt=JCM. Colin posed the question what might be made of *ACBC* (Anthony Colin Bruce Chapman). There were no polite suggestions.

David Benson, then motoring correspondent of the *Daily Express* was the first to tell me of Colin's death. The following day he published my tribute in his columns. It is still appropriate;

'Colin Chapman set the fashion and others followed, but were pale imitations. I regarded Colin as the outstanding racing car engineer and designer of this century. Through his genius the ordinary cars on the road benefited. His death marked the passing of an era.'

WALTER HAYES

I have often paid tribute to the role played by Walter Hayes, the former Vice-President of Ford's, in the changing face of Formula One racing. For many years we were on committees dealing with racing issues in which he showed the qualities that Sir Patrick Hennessy had recognised when he invited Walter to join the Ford Company after an outstanding editorship of the *Sunday Dispatch*. As Director of Ford Advanced Vehicles Ltd, he was instrumental in introducing the Ford-Cosworth Formula One engine by Keith Duckworth with chassis design by Mike Costain.

Walter shuns media publicity, preferring to influence in more discreet fashion. He has something of a dual personality in the motor-racing world. He presents an aloof exterior made complex by a chilling repression. He reminds me of a quince, a hard astringent fruit, concentrated in flavour, and somewhat restricted in appeal. In that sense he is a solitary. Like a well, if you drop a stone into it, you cannot get it out again. It is always tempting to look for the cause of a complex personality. In Walter's case it could be that he is a congenital intellectual.

In private life Walter is quite different. He hates the wrong type of publicity and resents the intrusion of the media into personal activities. The two are kept strictly apart. Only a few know the relaxed moods when he can be enormous fun, like the occasion when he joined us on an all-night celebrating party aboard a cruiser-steamer or helping Henry Ford II in his collection of ceramics. Walter's anecdotes are heightened by a habit of reaching the pay-off line with a dead-pan gravity.

His personal encouragement in establishing the International Grand Prix Medical Service was invaluable and helped to counter the Establishment's reluc-

tance to introduce badly needed changes. He was the motivating force behind the formation of the Jim Clark Foundation on which he invited me to serve as a Trustee.

In every sense Walter Hayes is a compelling personality, an admirable partner for Elizabeth, his charming, patient wife. He is a senior statesman of motor-racing.

PATRICK LINDSAY

The Honourable Patrick Linsay, second son of the 28th Earl of Crawford and 11th Earl of Balcarres, was a remarkable man. Endowed with immense energy, he pursued a wide range of interests. As senior Picture Director of Christie's, the fine art auctioneers, he conducted important sales of Old Masters with persuasive skill. In the 'seventies when prices peaked the £million-mark, it made news. In 1970 Lindsay sold a Velászquez for £2,310,000 and in 1985 knocked down Mantegna's '*Adoration of the Magi*' for an auction record of £8.1-million.

The knowledge and expertise marking his years at Christie's came from studying under the art historian and legendary nonagenarian, Bernhard Berenson. Ever mindful of that period, Lindsay used to say that the atmosphere of the Tuscany scene made a lasting impression on him. I was mindful of his remarks when I visited Settignano, situated on a hill overlooking vineyards amid the serenity of the Florentine countryside.

Berenson was surprisingly small, dressed in black coat with a clove buttonhole, goatee and jewelled hands. Awaiting the arrival of luncheon guests, small talk was eschewed, preferring instead to discuss the taste of other art collectors. The influence of this *grand seigneur* must have washed off on Lindsay's charming touch on the rostrum. It never deserted him. Once in Christie's before a pre-Raphaelite sale, I mentioned to him that we were interested in Millais's famous

'*The Grey Lady*' with its haunting, almost ghostly appeal.

The bidding began briskly then tailed off to a straight fight between myself and a London art dealer. Twice I reached my limit, but prodded by Jean, upped the bid. It was countered. After a long pause, during which Patrick concentrated and waited, I made my final offer. The hammer went before it could be bettered.

There were so many facets to Lindsay's life. At Eton he played cricket, the Field game and soccer, developed a passion for flying in the Oxford University Air Squadron, saw active service in Malaya with the Scots Guards. He enjoyed skiing, flying, travelling and motor-racing. The thrill of speed found an outlet in aeroplanes and historic cars.

The prized possessions in his collection were a 1940 Spitfire, an SE5 from the First World War and a rebuilt Hawker Fury. In 1948 he flew an exact replica of Blériot's cross-channel crossing in an identical time and wearing a tweed coat, collar and tie as worn by pioneering airmen. On this occasion the Muscular Dystrophy Fund benefited by the flight to the tune of several thousand pounds.

In motor-racing Lindsay's favourite was Remus, a two-litre supercharged ERA which with Romulus was owned and driven in the '30s by Prince Bira of Siam. Wearing what became an obligatory red shirt, Lindsay drove Remus in historic car races in Britain and Europe, winning the Richard Seaman Memorial Trophy nine times, registering 30 wins in 70 races, often touching speeds of 160 mph.

Another favourite in his collection of cars was a 1930 Rolls Royce Phantom, a gift from the Maharaja of Jaipur who stipulated that Lindsay should drive it home. This he did via the Khyber Pass and across desert tracks in Afghanistan. In auction in Los Angeles some twenty years ago he sold a 1946 Mercedes-Benz for 400,000 dollars.

For centuries, the Lindsays have made their mark in the arts, soldiering and sport. In a way this legacy continued when the calm of London's Park Lane was shattered by the roar of racing engines. An evening in 1994 saw the pavement outside The Dorchester packed with men in dinner-jackets and pretty girls in evening dresses sipping mugs of soup in freezing cold weather waiting for action from a line of Ferraris, Maseratis, Aston Martins, Porsche and E-Type Jaguars parked in Le Mans fashion. Prince Edward graced the occasion, which was the brainchild of Valentine Lindsay. He hoped it would be the forerunner of a future Grand Prix of Park Lane. Wishful thinking. Apart from John Prescott, the police are unconvinced. Neutral that night, traffic-wardens were missing, eyebrows were raised and tempers ruffled when traffic congestion brought buses, taxis and cars to a standstill. The cavalcade of racing cars zoomed round Hyde Park back to The Dorchester Club, where Valentine presided over a celebratory dinner.

ENZO FERRARI

Commendatore Enzo Ferrari was a man of power. His Maranello kingdom was a kingdom indeed. He was not manacled or chained. Broadly speaking he did what he liked. His decisions were sometimes eccentric, but sense of purpose never failed him. He had a unique association with the sport. Not only did he run the famous Alfa-Romeo team for nine years, but, after building his own factory, Ferrari sports cars and racing cars have at times dominated the World Championships, the 1998 revival of fortunes, Le Mans 24 Hours and the Mille Miglia, including six in a row, and more than 100 Grands Prix. A starting-grid of the dri-

Left: Always present for the practice days at Monza, Enzo would be absent for the Italian Grand Prix.

Above: Signora Laura Ferrari, lonely figure, almost sad while watching from the pit, in stark contrast to her matriarchal role in the Ferrari home.

vers who have been at the wheel of these Italian cars include almost every outstanding name, the latest being Michael Schumacher.

It is hard to describe Ferrari's influence to those who did not feel the impact of his personality. His presence had that intangible quality of weight, as distinct from build, by which the great always reveal themselves. He could be outrageous and uninhibited. He could pierce to the quick of an ulcer without bothering to administer sedation. Using a vein of ebullient, free-wheeling rancour, autocratic dictatorial exaggerations crept in. Such observations can be made about any organization governed and directed by a strong personality. Enzo Ferrari could go off the deep end, but it was not a vice in a sport that seldom ventures more than a toe into the water. The doyen of motor-racing could be conceded such latitude. The Commendatore was an Italian despot. He created an ambience in which, alongside driving intensity, even unreasonable anomalies were believable. Because of the tragic death of his only son Dino in 1956, there was no heir. One consolation is that the name of Ferrari will always be remembered and respected, not only in Italy, but throughout the motor-racing world.

COUNT WOLFGANG VON TRIPS

Count Wolfgang von Trips – elegant, polished, disciplined aristocrat, was somewhat apart in the Grand Prix world. There was no one quite like this tall blonde German. Vastly more intelligent than the sport he pursued, he was sensitive with a tough shell and a fine core. With his gifts and the possibility of profitable leisure, von Trips might have spent his time at his castle home in the forest near Cologne. That he should have looked after his family estates was one matter; that he should seek the title of World Champion was another. This last ambition explained the man. Throughout his racing career he displayed a desire to rattle the dice once more. He proved to himself that the man of taste, the virtuoso, could face the challenge of the Grand Prix circuits.

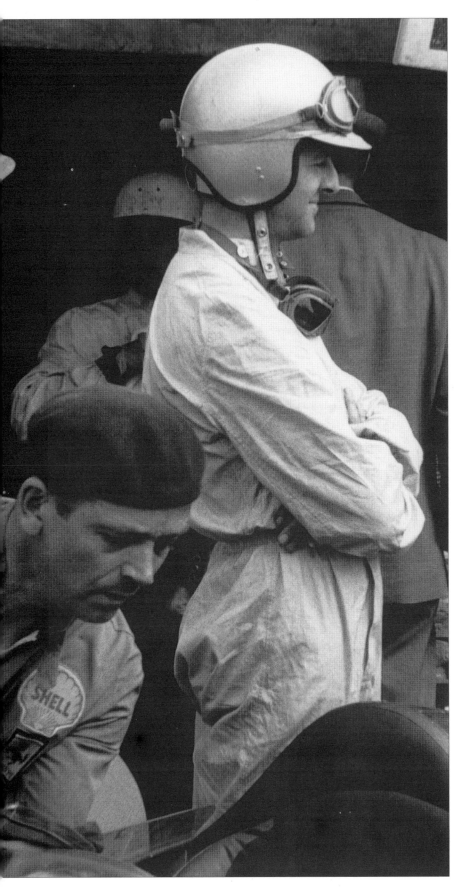

On the eve of the fateful 1961 Italian Grand Prix, we were with him in his castle home. They were anxious hours. It had been an eventful year. He won the Dutch Grand Prix at Zandvoort, the first German to win a Grand Epreuve since 1939, then added the British Grand Prix with an impressive drive in the rain at Aintree. It was the turn of Monza with a one-point lead in the Championship. That evening he recalled some of the highlights of his career. His reckless driving had given him a reputation of being accident prone. Maybe the luck would hold out. He recalled some previous disappointments, like driving a Formula One Lancia-Ferrari D50 in the Italian Grand Prix at Monza when the steering broke at high speed in practice. The car was wrecked but all he had were bruises. He was not so fortunate when his Ferrari hit Harry Schell's BRM in the opening lap. The German suffered a broken leg. He recalled vividly coming second to Taruffi in the 1957 Mille Miglia, and the bitterness of breaking down when leading on the last lap of the Targa Florio.

Conversation about past races was trivial alongside the prospects for the final race of the season which would decide the Championship. Monza was a combined road and high-speed circuit which had been boycotted the previous season by the British works-teams. Much depended on the reliability of the new V-8 Coventry-Climax power units and the debut of the BRM V-8. Ferrari took no chances. No fewer than six Ferraris were marshalled in front of the pits. Four 120-degree V-6s for Phil Hill, Von Trips, Ginther and Baghetti, a 60-degree V-6 for Ricardo Rodriguez, the sixth being used as a spare training car. Von Trips secured pole position with a lap of 2 min: 46.3 sec, or 134.541 mph. Ricardo had second fastest time. Phil Hill had a new engine the night before

Left: Count Wolfgang von Trips, one of the last aristocratic racing drivers

Right: Wolfgang's fearless style of driving appealed to the Commendatore, who tended to regard his drivers as dispensable.

the race. An innovation in practice sessions was the test on the banking for drivers new to Monza.

With alternate rows, the grid stretched over 300 yards. Earl Howe, President of the RAC, managed to get past the vigilant police and was handed the starting flag. On the tragic second lap, the field swept through the two right-handers, down to Vialone, then the straight to the Curvetta. Clark tried to overtake von Trip's Ferrari under braking. The cars touched at 149 mph and spun. Clark's car was almost undamaged. Von Trip's Ferrari went up the bank, ploughed along the spectator-lined fence and ricocheted back into the middle of the road. The German was thrown out and killed instantly. Fourteen spectators died. News of the accident was kept from the crowd. Unbelievably the race was allowed to continue.

I have never forgotten the tragedy of that day in Italy. Today's race incidents are insignificant by comparison. It was a personal tragedy that took a rare turn. It is hard for drivers to avoid dramatizing their lives, whether by over-living the part or becoming publicity conscious. Wolfgang von Trips was merely himself – a brave man who had come to terms, as we all may pray to do, with the thought that death could be near. In his career there was always a constant factor . . . a desire to be in two places at once and to do two things at the same time – he might even have had as his desire *wo du nicht bist, dort ist das Glück*.

His castle home still bore scars inflicted during the last war but gradually he was restoring it to its former dignity. The decorations, arrangement and choice of furniture and paintings were refreshingly individual. For centuries this had been the home of the Trips family. He was conscious of this tradition and the responsibilities that rested on his shoulders as the only son of elderly parents. He was full of plans for the development and improvement of the estate. Several of his ventures were profitable but this was as it should be. In our steel age, a man of means must command means if he is to survive.

I pay tribute to the memory of Wolfgang von Trips, the uncrowned World Champion of 1961.

DENIS JENKINSON

Denis Jenkinson was the answer to a cartoonist's prayer. Dwarflike with bristling red beard and thick spectacles, he was a familiar figure in the pit-lane looking for technical details which became telling comment in print. His opinions were respected, if at times his judgements were coloured by personal bias. He was not just an observant journalist; he could write, unlike most of his colleagues, from his personal experience. In the early days he was a motor-cycle ace to which could be added his memorable drive with Moss in the Mille Miglia.

One thing that used to irritate him was the campaign waged by the Grand Prix Drivers Association (GPDA) for improved safety standards for spectators and drivers. It was greeted with scorn, singling out Bonnier and Stewart for personal attack, caustically describing them as frightened nancy-boys. My response was to point out that such carps were academic. From the safety of the press box it was easy to be courageous, all they did was sit on their backsides. On the other hand, Jenks' opinions were good value . . .

Jenkinson is remembered for total commitment to motor-racing. It was his religion, but there was another side to his life. He spent a day with me at the Old Mill House in Cambridge. We sat in the secluded grounds and talked, or at least he did . . .

Left: Denis Jenkinson. Beneath a prickly exterior, he was at heart a loner, almost a recluse. He only came to life on a racing circuit. He had a somewhat Rabelaisian sense of humour.

JOHN & CHARLES COOPER

The unpretentious father-and-son partnership of John and Charles Cooper revolutionized motor-racing by achieving so much with so little. The set-up in Surbiton was simple. No publicity, no PRO, no glamour, apart from his fiancée Brady, handful of mechanics, designing staff of one draughtsman, no ultra-scientific experiments, just practical engineering directed by John Cooper aided and abetted by father Charles.

It began when the Coopers built midget cars that conformed with the formula for 500 cc racing cars and based on a Fiat '500' chassis with Speedway JAP engine. Front suspension units were united by a modified frame giving individual springing to each wheel. The engine was mounted behind the driver, solid axle through a Triumph motor-cycle clutch and gearbox, single chain sprocket, centralized steering column, short driving shafts with Ford universal joints allowed independent rear-suspension, wheels standard Fiat, brakes Lockheed-pattern hydraulic, engine air-cooled by an air vent tube along the chassis, developed 45 bph at 6,000 revs and weighed 550 lb unladen. Such was the beginning of the Cooper saga.

It became an evolutionary process. Recalling early races, the one that stands out was when the RAC took a one year experimental lease from the Air Ministry in October, 1948 for the Silverstone Aerodrome and planned a 500 cc race to precede the Grand Prix. Entry was limited to 30 cars, race-distance 50

Below: Charles Cooper worrying in case he had miscalculated.

Below: Bruce McLaren and John Cooper - temperamentally attuned.

miles, prize-money £50 first, £30 second, £20 pounds third. Earl Howe started the race. The first four places were taken by Coopers. The car was to become a training exercise for potential Grand Prix drivers like Peter Collins and Stirling Moss. Commercially it made sense. If you fixed the engine yourself, a racing car could be bought for £500. Motor-racing had arrived for the small-purse enthusiast.

Similar principles were adopted for the Formula Two class by fitting into the same chassis 996cc and 1,098cc JAP engines for hill-climb events. The JAP was later replaced by 1/2-litre Norton motor-cycle engine. 1952 saw the début of a Cooper with a 2-litre Bristol engine mounted at the front. With Mike Hawthorn, Coopers had arrived. Progress accelerated with the incorporation and development of the Coventry-Climax engine, first used by the fire brigade as a mobile pump. In Cooper sports cars its capacity was only 1,100cc, but when Coventry-Climax put a 1 1/2-litre unit in the Cooper Formula Two, rear-engined single-seater, the results were sensational. On occasions it was superior to the 2 1/2-litre Formula One cars. The classic instance was the 1958 Argentine Grand Prix when Rob Walker's 1,960cc Cooper-Climax driven by Stirling Moss beat the 2 1/2-litre Ferraris.

In retrospect there were several highlights, like the Monaco Grand Prix when the rookie Jack Brabham took the wheel of a Cooper with a 2-litre Coventry Climax engine and alloy-spoked Minilite wheels. With three laps to go, the Australian was in third place when the fuel pump mounting failed. He pushed the car over the line to take sixth place and earned for Coopers, and himself, their first World Championship point.

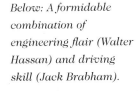

Below: A formidable combination of engineering flair (Walter Hassan) and driving skill (Jack Brabham).

Below: Leonard Lee who, with Walter Hassan, made the Coventry Climax engine a world beater, ably backed up by engineer Harry Mundy.

In 1958 the FIA decreed that Formula One cars should run on Av-Gas aviation fuel, a ruling that gave an advantage for smaller, lighter cars like Coopers. The Climax engine produced 180 bhp, which was fractionally less than the previous alcohol-based solvents. Stretched to 2.2-litres, it showed 194bhp. Stirling Moss confirmed its competitiveness by winning the Argentine Grand Prix. Then in 1959 Coopers introduced the Coventry-Climax 2.5-litre unit that developed 250 bhp.

In so many ways the Cooper era was remarkable. David and Goliath duels are compelling, especially when fiction becomes fact.

Charles Cooper had an interesting background: Kay Don's mechanic, racing driver, pilot, designer of aeroplanes and racing cars, he helped to shape the team. At times could be blunt but had a dry sense of humour. Stubborn when it came to change. Progressive decisions were motivated by John, who was professional in all that he did. When Leonard Lee, managing-director of Coventry-Climax, came on the scene, their combined enthusiasm and skills earned double wins in the Formula One World and Manufacturers Championships. Together they made racing history. It came as a shock when Lee announced that his firm was withdrawing from racing. Apart from Cooper, teams like Lotus, Brabham and Bowmaker-Lola had become dependent on their V-8 engines that won no fewer than 22 Grands Prix. The reason for the decision was economic. In spite of establishing British supremacy in Grand Prix racing, the cost of design and development had meant financial loss. The firm felt it could not subsidize motor-racing.

A proud chapter had ended, many memories remain. The Coopers were solid characters with a conservative outlook. In lighter vein I recall a Gala Dinner in the Hotel de Paris after the Monaco Grand Prix. John, thoroughly enjoying the meal, remarked how tender the chicken was. I mentioned the succulent dish was frogs' legs, whereupon John was almost ill on the spot. Such delicacies were not popular at home.

GRAHAM HILL

Seven years of close contact with Graham Hill during his stay with BRM made me a connoisseur of reality. During that time he changed in marked degree. In the early days he used to get ulcerously edgy before a race, especially if it rained. He was not a 'natural' driver like Clark, but developed the hard way by concentrated effort. In time his style matured and grew more relaxed, almost aloof.

Externally he was emphatically the professional, as smooth and hard as perspex. He analysed himself as lethally as he analysed his opponents. Extremely self-assured, he had an intimate grasp of the English art of one-up-manship. He needed his public as much as any other man who goes surf-riding on enthusiasm. Emotion of any kind he expressed by thrusting out his chin and knitting his eyebrows. He was one of those curious Englishmen who are almost concretely English in appearance. His features, personal mannerisms like a brush at his moustach, reticent clothes, handkerchief surreptitiously tucked away in his pocket, well-scrubbed face, suggested an Army officer on leave or a school master fresh from morning roll-call. He attempted to be with it by growing his hair exceptionally long. It did not work. Away from the track he looked like a militant plain-clothes friar in need of a tonsure.

Physically he could cope with the strain. A younger generation of drivers in spite of their painstaking efforts were still a long way short of his resilient driving,

Right: Graham Hill adopts a Rodin- style pose.

Above: Graham relaxing in the garden of his Finchley home after returning victorious from the Indianapolis 500. Henry Taylor on grass, Graham, Jim Clark and Colin Chapman.

judgement and skill. But once the edge had worn off and lesser fry were beating him he should have withdrawn. I prefer to see a great driver in the highest reaches of his art, not splashing around in its shallows. Sadly it all ended on Saturday, November 30, 1975, when a light aircraft crashed on a golf course near Elstree Aerodrome. Poor visibility, possibly pilot error, caused the death of all its occupants – Graham Hill, Tony Brise and members of his team who were returning from testing on the Paul Ricard circuit in France. It was a tragic loss. There was no one quite like Graham Hill. My praise may seem exaggerated but I have never met anyone in the sport who was fairer or more sincere. Abroad he was motor-racing's finest ambassador. I only wish that his talented son, Damon, was more like his father.

ROB WALKER

Everything I have written about Robert Ramsey Campbell Walker is still applicable. He was the most eminent private entrant in motor-racing. His association with the sport extends to some 55 years. At the outset he raced himself. In 1939 with Ian Connell as co-driver in a 3.5 litre Type 135 Delahaye, he finished 8th in the Le Mans 24-Hour race with the added distinction of being the only man ever

to drive in this event garbed in a city suit. Marriage put a stop to racing. It became the role of entrant. Among those who drove for him were such names as Jack Brabham, Tony Rolt, Tony Brooks, Reg Parnell, Peter Collins, Maurice Trintignant, Joakim Bonnier, Roy Salvadori and Stirling Moss. Rob is also the only private entrant to have won World Championship races.

Throughout all this, Rob presided and directed in genial fashion. He was an odd mixture and still is a bundle of contradictions. He speaks directly in a drawl that sounds hardly like Oxford but is in fact Cambridge. He is in no sense loquacious but can indulge in healthy glottal wheedling. He gives the impression of immaculate precision and aplomb, plus a bland knowing presence that is no more than a screen behind which lurks an enquiring, shrewd and sensitive mind. His prestige remained steadily high with several ups and very few downs. He was very much in demand by all race organizers. His tiptoe enthusiasm has not waned. The absence of insularity is the yardstick of his stature. He is one of the few who still regards motor-racing as a sport with rules of conduct that should be observed. The current state of the sport with its commercialism and inflated contracts is censured. We share one dislike – I find Murray Walker tiresome and irritating. By all means watch the races on television but turn off the hysterical commentary and listen to the radio.

Above: Rob and Betty Walker were passionate in their approach to motor-racing. Among the many drivers who competed in their cars, Jo Siffert was one of the favourites.

INNES IRELAND

When Innes Ireland retired the racing world lost its last extrovert. The mental picture I have of this turbulent personality was of outsize energy and enthusiasm that never came to fruition. Some drivers have a small talent which they believe to be big. There are several of this type on today's grids. Ireland had a big talent which he chose to be part-idle. He could have achieved so much more had he imposed self-discipline. When racing he had no private property. Everything about him was public and he was open daily. Courage and insensitivity are said to be twins. Both were present in Innes. He reminded me of the man who said, 'When I'm unhappy, I can't work. When I'm happy, I don't need work. When I don't need work, I'm unhappy'. Innes was a mixture of extremes. He could drive brilliantly, then a moment of irritation would ruin everything. He always gave value for money. Spectators loved him. He was a tonic to mechanics but at times could send team managers round the bend. He was immensely popular with his fellow-drivers. He had a reputation of being a hard man to beat, but always scrupulously fair. Crash after crash dented his body, but not his spirit. He not only seemed more eloquent, more joyous than any other driver, but was particularly available to all and everyone – utterly without pose. In 1961 he won the United States Grand Prix in a Lotus. It was his first and only championship win; it was also the first championship victory that year for Lotus. In spite of the success, Chapman dropped him from the works team in favour of Clark. The decision rankled with Innes for many years.

Retirement as driver led to another career as Sports Editor of *Autocar*. After a somewhat hesitant start, his style improved, likewise fact verification, with the result that his columns were witty, readable and authoritative. His death after a lengthy illness was a shock. In an age of supremely careful people searching for the security of personal happiness, Innes lived without sense, without an analyst and provoked astonishment and affection from everyone.

TAZIO NUVOLARI

Tazio Nuvolari ranked as one of the greatest drivers of all time. His inimitable driving style was demonstrated in the middle thirties when the new Mercedes-Benz and Auto-Union cars, supported by the Nazi government, out-classed his Alfa-Romeo. He was the only driver to challenge their superiority. Reckless courage compensated in part for the missing horsepower. He had a series of appalling crashes, but somehow survived. It was part of his nature. He signed up with Auto-Union but only found success on the difficult circuits. His courage was legendary. He must have been a difficult boy to control. His exploits included jumping off a roof with a home-made parachute, escaping with bruises. Another exploit was assembling a dismantled Blériot aeroplane, trying to take off and hitting a haystack which burst into flames. He was lucky enough to escape with only an injured shoulder.

Nuvolari's tally of victories was remarkable. The 1930 Mille Miglia was typical. With only a few miles to go he closed the gap on his rival Varzi, switched off his head-lights, then took the lead with a couple of miles to go. This rivalry continued in 1931 when Nuvolari won the Targa Florio. 1932 continued this winning streak with the Monaco Grand Prix, Targa Florio, Italian Grand Prix, the Prince of Piedmont Race, the Ciano Cup and the Acerbo Cup, earning the title of Champion of Italy. 1933 was just as eventful. Driving an Alfa-Romeo, he collected the Tunis Grand Prix, the Mille Miglia, the Circuit of Alexandria, the Eifelrennet, Nîmes Grand Prix and Le Mans 24-Hours. At Monaco he renewed rivalry with Varzi's Bugatti. The lead changed on every lap. Nuvolari's car blew up and burst into flames. Extinguished, the little Italian pushed the car to the finish and collapsed some 200 yards from it, only to find he had been disqualified.

His charmed life was put to the test at Alessandria. Count Trossi's car developed mechanical trouble. Taking evasive action, the car veered across the track and slammed into a tree. Nuvolari's right leg was broken. The news that Varzi had won in Tripoli made him determined to race at Avus the following week. Encased in a plaster cast, he finished a creditable fourth in spite of considerable pain.

1935 brought personal satisfaction. He went back to the Alfa-Romeo team managed by Ferrari. In spite of the superiority of Mercedes-Benz and Auto-Union, he won the Pau Grand Prix, the Bergamo Cup, Ciano Cup and races at Turin, Modena and Biella, and then achieved the near-impossible in the German Grand Prix at Nürburgring. On the last lap he beat Manfred von Brauchitsch's Mercedes. He regarded this victory as his greatest. In 1936 he again had a crash at Tripoli with a burst tyre. Broken ribs in the inevitable plaster corset, he ignored the doctor's advice and raced the following day, finishing seventh. The saga continued. Victory after victory punctuated by his injuries. He seemed indestructible. His last race was at Monte Pellegrino which he won. From that point his health deteriorated and he died at his luxurious villa at Mantua, at the age of sixty. His last wish was carried out. He was buried in the renowned yellow jersey, blue trousers and helmet.

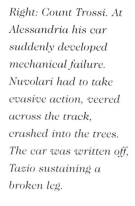

Right: Count Trossi. At Alessandria his car suddenly developed mechanical failure. Nuvolari had to take evasive action, veered across the track, crashed into the trees. The car was written off, Tazio sustaining a broken leg.

COUNT GODIN DE BEAUFORT

Count Carel Godin de Beaufort was a true amateur. Tall, massively built, he did battle in an out-dated orange four-cylinder Porsche. Against him were cars of far greater power, yet such was his dogged persistence that time and again the aged machine would finish, whilst his rivals dropped out or blew up. In 1962 he out-paced and outdrove the Porsche works flat-eight machines. Had it not been for a mishap at Watkins Glen, he would have been classified as a finisher in every race counting towards the World Championship.

Carel de Beaufort was full of mannerisms. Invariably he drove in his stockinged feet. Even at moments of pressure during a Grand Prix, he would suddenly wave to a friend alongside the track. He hated half measures. Everything had to be all or nothing. At one time he became overweight. Dieting was prescribed. In a surprisingly short time 70lb had been lost. He stayed with us in Cambridge for a few days. On arrival he opened a briefcase. Inside were scores of tiny bottles containing pills. At the end of his visit, I knew everything there was to know about calories. On another occasion he was guest at our daughter's 21st birthday party. His technique was quick, like his driving. Some distance away at a different table was the attractive daughter of the Vice-Chancellor. The following morning she received a sheaf of roses with de Beaufort's compliments.

Motor-racing was de Beaufort's life. He enriched the sport with his exuberant presence. His home, Maarsbergen Castle in Holland, bore evidence of his enthusiasm. His study held shelves of trophies, one of the most precious being the trophy give to him by the Grand Prix Drivers Association, a recognition by fellow

Left: Count Godin de Beaufort. Like von Trips, a breed now lost to the sport.

Right: Earl Howe -
courteously abrasive,
but used charm to get
his own way.

drivers of his vastly improved driving. It made one realize that to some, motor-racing was a sport to be enjoyed. Sadly, luck deserted him in the 1962 German Grand Prix. Trying desperately to make his old Porsche go fast enough to qualify, he overdid it at the Bergwerk corner and hit a tree, receiving head and spine injuries. After the race I went to the hospital, only to find he had been taken by helicopter to Düsseldorf. When I arrived it was to learn there was no hope. His high noon kept all the freshness of the morning – and he died there – never knowing the disillusionments of today.

EARL HOWE

Earl Howe, who died in 1964 at the age of 80, was a leading racing driver of the 1930's. He began competitive racing in 1928 aged 44, a distinctive figure with brilliant blue helmet, racing overalls, and an outsize Oxford blue umbrella to shield him from rain or sun on the starting-grid.

In 1931 he acquired the famed 1.5-litre Delage from Malcolm Campbell and won his class in the Grand Prix de Dieppe that year. Monza was not so fortunate. On braking, the servo jammed – all four wheels locked. The car spun backwards into the trees, completely destroyed, but the driver was unhurt. I remember the wreckage being dumped in the mews garage by the Dorchester Hotel in London.

1932 saw Howe at the wheel of a 2.3-litre green Bugatti that finished fourth in the Monaco Grand Prix behind Nuvolari, Caracciola and Fagioli. 1931 saw him win the Gold Star handicap at Brooklands beating John Cobb and Tim Birkin. Le Mans that year with Birkin as co-driver proved an eventful race. After six hours they had overtaken the Aston Martins, Mercedes and Talbot to take second place. Six hours later they led and never lost it, claiming the fastest 24 Hours on record

*Left: Earl Howe delivers
a confidential aside to
Wilkie Wilkinson, who is
still active as he
approaches the century
mark.*

with a combined average speed of 78.13mph. In 1936 he tried his luck in a British car by buying an ERA. A feat that gave considerable satisfaction was clocking a 108.27-mph lap at Brooklands in a Lagonda at the age of 54.

Howe exercised considerable influence as President of the British Racing Drivers Club, Chairman of the RAC Competitions Committee and vice-president of the CSI. His contributions were always incisive and to the point as befitted his ancestor, the first Lord Howe, victor of the Glorious First of June. He served with distinction in the Navy throughout the First World War and on HMS *Queen Elizabeth* in the Dardanelles Campaign.

As he walked about the pit area like an ambulent cigar, he looked indestructible. One of the last gentlemen amateurs of the motor-racing scene.

STIRLING MOSS

Stirling Moss was born into motor-racing. His father, Alfred, a dental surgeon, drove the Barber-Warnock Fords on two occasions at Indianapolis and set up the first 100-mph lap made by a Ford at Brooklands, whilst his mother, Aileen, had many successes in rallies and trials. Moss was immensely proud of his parents and particularly of his sister, Pat Moss-Carlsson, who with Ann Riley (formerly Wisdom) outdrove all the men over four days and nights in the Liège-Rome-Liège, the world's toughest event, at the wheel of that muscular car, the Big

Right: Alfred Moss was often accompanied by his wife Aileen. Both were strong characters who made their presence felt in the pits. Both had distinguished motor-racing backgrounds.

Right: Stirling Moss, unquestionably the finest driver to miss the World Championship title. His flair was remarkable. Had machinery been more reliable the story would have been different. Today he is the natural spokesman for the sport.

Healey. Add to that her success in showjumping – a remarkable family.

At the wheel of a racing car, Stirling became a legend. The ironic part is that in spite of so many brilliant victories, the ultimate accolade eluded him. It was unfortunate that his heyday coincided with the era of the greatest of all drivers, Juan Manuel Fangio, three times – 1955, 1956 and 1957 Stirling was runner-up in the World Championship to the Argentinian. Success in those days was tough with grids of Villoresi, Nuvolari, Ascari, Musso, Gonzalez, Hawthorn and Collins. By comparison the drivers today are selling-platers.

There are many memories of Stirling's brilliance, such as his sensational win in the Mille Miglia that broke all records, followed by victory in the Targa Florio with co-driver, Peter Collins, and in particular his inspired driving in Rob Walker's Cooper-Climax. I think also of his handling of the BRM when he claimed second place in the British Grand Prix at Aintree and the magnificent win in the same event driving a Vanwall. Success in the World Championship came to an abrupt end in 1962.

In the Formula One race at Goodwood on Easter Monday, Stirling was driving a Lotus-Climax V8. Mechanical troubles had meant two pit stops that left him down the field, well behind Graham Hill in a BRM. Coming out of the Fordwater bend, his car went off the track at more than 100mph and crashed into an earthbank. Trapped in the car with severe head injuries, Stirling was in a coma for 32 days with right side paralysed. Recovery was slow. Competitive racing was over. Time has worked wonders. Although no longer flamboyant and extroverted, Stirling is now the veteran ambassador of the sport, a reminder of the golden years of motorracing.

Right: Stirling stepping-it out in the rain. The action typified his manner: short, over-energetic, in some ways almost ascetic. His home in Shepherd's Market in London has every possible labour-saving gadget. Aficionado of sportscar racing, in which he was supreme.

GERALD LASCELLES

The Honourable Gerald Lascelles, cousin of the Queen, exercised a practical influence on motor-racing in his capacity as President of the British Racing Drivers Club. On the death of Earl Howe, Gerald became only the third in thirty-seven years to be elected to this office.

I had many dealings with Gerald. He was an odd mixture, at time over-dogmatic. Took a firm stand against what he considered to be negative caution. There was no doubting his sincerity, even though at times he was too uncompromising in his views. Such forthright attitude to motor-racing was shared by Tony Rolt with whom he served in the British Army of Occupation in post-war Germany. In many ways they were kindred spirits. Rolt, who was his Company Commander in the Rifle Brigade, won the Le Mans 24 Hours Race in 1953. Gerald held office for 27 years before retiring to a château in the Dordogne region of France at the end of 1991 with his wife Lisa.

Left: The Honourable Gerald Lascelles - for many years President of the British Racing Drivers Club and outspoken administrator. Very popular.

JIM CLARK

When Jim Clark died in a crash at Hockenheim, Grand Prix racing lost some of its magnetism. Jim Clark avoided the poseur pitfalls. He was just himself. Nothing strained, technical equipment immaculate, he had no superior on the track. 1965 was a peak year. He won the World Championship for the second time with a sequence of six wins in a row and became the first British driver to win the Indianapolis 500 at the record speed of 150.686-mph. The virtuosity of Clark's driving put him in a category of his own. In my estimate he ranks second to the world's finest driver, Juan Manuel Fangio.

I accepted without hesitation the invitation to become one of the three Trustees of the Jim Clark Foundation. It was a practical way of keeping alive the memory of this great driver.

LOUIS CHIRON

Many people recall Chiron as the eccentric Commissaire General of the Monaco Grand Prix, an appointment made by Prince Rainier. As starter of the race he was regarded as a suicide risk. Year after year he just managed to skip out of the way of the accelerating cars. He controlled everything and everybody with voice and flag. His talent was irascible, but, in spite of Gallic eruptions, he discharged his duties efficiently. His manner suggested that the end of the world, when it arrived, would be announced in French. But, on their own, such colourful recollections do not do him justice as an outstanding racing driver.

Born on August 2nd, 1899, Chiron worked at the Hotel de Paris. At the end of World War One he was chauffeur to Marshal Pétain. His first appearance in competitive racing was in 1923 in a Brescia Bugatti without much luck; then four years later he bought the first supercharged 2.3-litre type 35B Bugatti and had an impressive drive in the Spanish Grand Prix. In the same year finished fourth in the British Grand Prix at Brooklands behind the formidable Delage team. Further successes followed, including the European Grand Prix at Monza when he beat Campari and Nuvolari with a record average of 99.4 mph over the 373-mile circuit. Success followed success. In conjunction with Anthony Noghes, he organized and planned the first Monaco Grand Prix. The first race in 1929 was won by Williams. Dreyfus denied him victory the following year by 22 seconds. Victory came in 1931 at the wheel of his Type 51 Bugatti. The war interrupted his chain of wins, but the vein continued. His last major victory was the Grand Prix of France in 1949, then a final fling with a class win in the Mille Miglia at the age of 58.

It was a proud record, yet somehow we remember him by eccentricities as race starter. In spite of the dramatics, there were no hitches. Maybe unorthodox, but far better than the current system prefaced with the idiotic shriek on television urging viewers to watch the lights!

JUAN MANUEL FANGIO

Juan Manuel Fangio was the greatest driver of all time. In the 'fifties he dominated Grand Prix racing, winning five Formula One World Championships before retiring at the age of 54. The years never bothered him. He was 47 when he made his début on European circuits. Success came in the works teams of Alfa-Romeo, Mercedes, Ferrari and Maserati. A few statistics show the extent of his domination. He won 24 of his 51 Grand Prix races, 48 times on the front row of the grid, 28 times held pole position, fastest race lap 23 times.

Right: The German Grand Prix of 1957 demonstrated Fangio's incredible concentration and stamina. At 48.5 seconds behind the leaders because of a pit stop, he reacted by breaking the lap record several times before catching up with Mike Hawthorn and Peter Collins as they exited a corner behind the pits. He bisected the two rivals to take the chequered flag. It was a glorious display under relentless pressure.

He recalled how the intensity of racing in his heyday was such that 30 of his fellow drivers were killed. Of the current drivers, he regretted the tendency to whinge when things went wrong, and deplored their outbursts of temper that brought the sport into disrepute. Off and on the tracks, Juan was the diplomat, hard to beat but scrupulously fair. He was immensely popular in England in spite of the fact that he never mastered English and was dependent on interpreters. His charisma did not need words.

KEN TYRRELL

I one wrote that Ken Tyrrell took some understanding, rather like getting to grips with the Royal Albert Hall. I referred to his wry, laconic, pungent sense of humour that could be highly personal. Voice whirred and buzzed like an engine that once revved-up cannot be switched off. Deep lines of concentration bisected his forehead like a highway. He was a familiar landmark in the pits – gawky and angular, with large feet, untidy hair, mouthful of teeth, accusatory eyes. When amused he was an engulfing spectacle, the cachinnation of his laughter was infectious. When

Left: Ken Tyrrell is remembered as a gawky, blunt, dishevelled figure who larded the pits with disarming candour. No airs and graces, just plain honesty and a workmanlike approach.

talking he stoops and peers into the ear of the individual at the receiving end. Tyrrell had the knack of getting the best out of his drivers. Quick to spot talent, particularly Jackie Stewart whom he earmarked as potential World Championship material. The prediction was right, with World Championship and Constructor's titles.

Lean times followed. His cars slipped to the back of the grid. The quality of drivers mediocre. It seemed a logical step to sell out, the buyers being British American Tobacco. It must have been a terrific wrench, but Ken is too much of a realist to hanker for the good times. He is sadly missed, rough, tough, but sincere. Unlike some of his colleagues, he is proud of the traditions of the sport.

SIR FRANK WILLIAMS

Among the many personalities who have enriched the sport, Frank Williams is a man apart. In the pits surrounded by activity and turmoil, he sits in a wheelchair, silent, hands leather-gloved rest on his knees, wearing headphones, intently watching television monitors of the race. Manner glacial. His disability is the result of an accident when returning from testing on Le Castelet circuit in the South of France.

Left: Following the announcement of the names in the New Year Honours List, it is now a privilege to acknowledge the astounding courage under adversity of Sir Frank Williams. What he has achieved has given encouragement to countless others who have similar handicaps.

His passenger, Peter Windsor, later told me what happened. Possibly through going too fast, the car went out of control, left the road, somersaulted, and plunged down the bank. Windsor crouched into a ball, protected his head, and waited for the crash-landing. He was fortunate, but not so Frank. His spine was fractured at the seventh and eighth vertebrae, both legs, torso and arms paralysed. He was left a paraplegic.

For someone who was a fitness fanatic, an active sportsman who ran six miles a day, passionate about motor-racing, on the verge of real success, it was a physical and mental disaster that would have broken the spirit of most men. At least he could speak; his brain was incisive. Gradually he came to terms with the condition. Rehabilitation exercises and the reassuring support of his wife, Virginia, helped the resumption of a racing career, obviously with physical limitations, but able to keep an all-seeing eye on every aspect of race-preparations, tactics and shrewd assessment of driver skills, traits that stood him in good stead when he raced on a shoestring budget. They were tough times sustained by optimism.

Frank was the life and soul of any party. I recall him in St. Jovite, Canada, giving a hand to our mechanics unloading the BRMs, sitting on a bank afterwards, chewing chocolate wholemeal biscuits which he said were his basic diet. After the accident, the technical expertise of men like Patrick Head was invaluable. Frank's highly successful role was wooing potential sponsors, initially gentlemen of Arab extraction, and engine manufacturers. It became a saga of incredible success with World Championship titles, record-breaking nine Constructor's Cups, and a string of brilliant drivers- Nigel Mansell, Alain Prost, Jacques Villeneuve, Damon Hill, and his greatest discovery, the Brazilian Ayrton Senna. Frank has a reputation of being unpredictable about renewing drivers' contracts even after their skills produce championship titles. Contractual disputes about terms of dealing with prima-donnas caused surprise decisions. His attitude is justified. Drivers, however good, are dispensable. The car and engine development are all-important. This policy paid rich dividends.

Since the days when Frank had to watch every penny, he is now a multi-millionaire, yet, in spite of the luxuries that such a fortune can give, I am sure he would forego them all if only his health and mobility were restored. As it is, he can indulge in other things. One is an insatiable craving to keep changing his home...It is fortunate that Virginia's philosophy accepts such moves as a challenge to her decorating, furnishing and imaginative tastes. As there are no worries about finding money to pay the rent, it has become a spiral of prestigious selection. It has occured seven times in 21 years. It began in 1977 with the Old Rectory at Aston Tirrold then, in sequence, Battle House three years later, a sprawling 19th-century house in Goring, Oxfordshire (c. £280,000); 1986, Boxford House, in Boxford, near Newbury (c. £500,000); the Old Rectory in East Ilsley (c.£600,000); 1990, Craven House in Hamstead Marshall near Newbury (c. £800,000); 1993, Stargroves, an atmospheric mansion at East Woodhay, near Newbury, former home of Mick Jagger (c. £2-million); 1998, eight miles away to Inholmes at Woodlands St Mary near Hungerford (c. £4-million).

Such a restless search to establish roots for the meaningful future is not a good sign. Once established, a sense of permanence can develop and mature, otherwise it becomes an Ecclestone-symptom that knows the price of everything and the value of nothing. Such an attitude is not to be envied. On the contrary, it seems pointless. I prefer to think of Frank as someone who commands admiration, not for his financial acquisitions, but for his sheer courage under adversity.

JOAKIM BONNIER

Jo Bonnier was born in Stockholm on the 31st January, 1930. He left school at 19, joined the Navy, eventually getting a commission. His father, a professor at Stockholm University, persuaded him to enter Oxford University and read English Literature. He went on to Paris and joined the influential family firm of publishers. He became multilingual in French, English, Italian, Spanish and German, married Marianne, and lived in Lausanne, Switzerland. Had he wished they could have lived comfortably in a semi-academic cultural background. Instead he chose the competitive arena of motor-racing.

In this activity the bearded Swede had the anonymity of granite. As a Formula One driver he was perennially absorbing. The skill was there, but concentration wavered. It was like marking an examination paper of a brilliant student on what he *might* have written. It all came good in the 1959 Dutch Grand Prix at Zandvoort. He registered BRM's first win in the World Championship, and a memorable victory for the Swede. It was his only triumph in the Championship.

For several years I worked closely with him in the Grand Prix Drivers Association of which he was founder and president. His invaluable efforts to make circuits safer have never been fully acknowledged. Memories are short. Killed in the Le Mans 24 Hours, his Lola somersaulted over the barrier into the trees. Others, like Jackie Stewart, took the credit for Jo's pioneering policies. The Press became

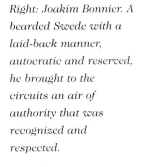

Right: Joakim Bonnier. A bearded Swede with a laid-back manner, autocratic and reserved, he brought to the circuits an air of authority that was recognized and respected.

hostile and accused him and those who supported the campaign, of being cardboard heroes . . . ironic coming from hacks who criticized from a safe distance. These contentious issues were eventually confirmed by officialdom and circuit owners alike.

Away from the circuits and wrangling, Jo was relaxed and interesting. It is rare to find a racing driver who had such a width of interests. Often their brains are between their neck and their knees.

JACKIE STEWART

On rare occasions a young man appears on the circuits and immediately impresses by his handling of a racing car. This was true of Jackie Stewart. Form shown with the Ecurie Ecosse team and Ken Tyrrell's Formula Three cars, was confirmed behind the wheel of a BRM, the ultimate in Formula One machinery.

His confident self-assurance was remarkable, particularly on this début in the opening practice laps at Nürburgring, a stern examination for veterans, let alone rookies. With unruffled temperament, he was a 'natural'. It was all there. Sucess followed success, plus World Championhsip honours. It was a sad day when he retired, a decision influenced by the deaths of close friends like Jim Clark, Jochen Rindt and François Cevert. His tally was impressive. Twenty-seven Grand Prix victories from 99 starts.

As an individual Jackie went through several phases. At the outset we at

Right: Driving skill was matched by Stewart's stamina as a non-stop chatterer, much of it needing an interpreter. He was a 'natural' driver who made everything seem easy, almost effortless. It was a privilege to have him in the BRM team.

Right: This photograph at the height of Jackie's fame is in sharp contrast to his current staid image, but underneath he is still the true son of his race.

BRM enjoyed his quirky brand of Scottish humour. He impressed everyone by his stamina. He never stopped talking. The only person able to stem the flow was his wife, Helen, then a bank clerk in a Glasgow bank. At the counter I am sure verbose customers were discouraged. Racing success changed their way of life. Staying with us in Cambridge, he admitted it was difficult to settle. When away he wanted to be home and vice versa. He became less restless after buying a semi-detached Victorian house in a Glasgow suburb. But success meant upheaval. The family moved to Geneva because of income-tax benefits. Change of lifestyle was perhaps not so welcome for Helen who had language problems, but, out of character, Jackie adopted a trendy role, with long shoulder-length unkempt hair and mod clothes, as if anticipating the taste of Ruud Gullit. Not that it mattered. We all have to grow up.

It did not affect his brilliant driving, on a par with Fangio and Clark. His other contribution to the sport was campaigning for circuit safety. With his electric personality he was an excellent ally, whose contribution was especially valuable after the lamentable death of Joakim Bonnier.

With advancing years, Jackie has become more restrained. Never afraid to take up a challenge, he has launched the Stewart racing team with his son Paul and Ford power. Whether it was a wise decision remains to be seen. What is certain is that Jackie has total support from the motor racing public.

Starting from scratch, Jackie gave himself a 5-year programme to become fully competitive. The third year has provided improved engine power, but reliability is suspect. Morale is high, and both drivers are confident. It will be a wonderful moment when they make the winners' podium.

3
'Fings Ain't What they Used to Be

Since BRM withdrew, I have viewed the racing scene with interest and no little concern. Technical developments over the past decade have revolution-ized the sport. Increased commercial activities have hastened the change, with sponsorship demands and tussles to secure placement-advertising within television camera range. Another irritation is the way fans are being ripped-off by the inflated prices of endorsed sporting equipment. Motivation is greed, sheer greed and to hell with ethics. The disturbing fact is that this trend has become accepted as the norm.

The clock cannot be turned back, but the purist has a duty to point out that motor-racing has a proud tradition untarnished by such tactics. Much of the former spontaneous sparkle has gone, replaced by clinical rules. Even the moments after victory are arranged. The set-piece of champagne soaking, caps worn showing sponsor-logos to the cameras, compulsory press briefings, drivers taking refuge in motorhomes, then jetting away before the spectators have left the circuits. Circus-type television presentation with over-dramatic build-up interspersed with advertising breaks. High pressure stuff that leaves those who fail with a sense of failure.

Above: Congested, shared pits at Monaco. No privacy for drivers or mechanics, an absence of motorhomes. Unthinkable today, but these were once integral features of the Monaco Grand Prix.

Right: Of all circuits none can rival the setting of Monte Carlo with its backcloth of towering white and ochre buildings rising in tiers to jagged mountain peaks touched by drifting clouds.

Psychiatrists analyse such symptoms. They maintain that conditions today make people feel like losers, their consensus being that we are now anything like up to ten times more likely to be depressed than we were in 1950. Oliver James in his book *Britain on the Couch*, argues that it is the way we live rather than our genes that induces in our bodies low levels of seratonin, the 'happiness' brain chemical! Michael Argyle, Emeritus Professor of Psychology at Oxford adds his bit, 'Those who value money most are less satisfied and in poorer mental health because money provides only superficial kinds of satisfaction'. Theoretically he may be right, but I have yet to see the likes of Ron Dennis, Bernie Ecclestone or Michael Schumacher showing such symptoms.

The argument put forward that economic problems, huge unemployment, and the Cold War threat created a cloud of depression is not entirely true. On the contrary the mood was cheerful, certainly when it came to the atmosphere at Grands Prix. Sceptics disagree. The so-called golden era of motor-racing is a

myth. Conditions today, they point out, are far better. Safety standards improved, no fatalities, fewer injuries, what more can drivers and spectators want? Few would dispute such facts, yet the fact remains that in those turbulent days some forty years ago, there were many lighter moments. As an instance, when the German Grand Prix was held in Berlin, Russian troops patrolled the Memorial in front of the Brandenburg Gate with warning notices that here was the border-line dividing East and West Germany. In spite of military domination, there was spontaneous enjoyment at Avus, often fuelled by trivialities like a psychological safety-valve. Overall the past had compensations that do not exist today. Put it to the test by recalling some of the preliminaries to the Monaco Grand Prix, the most glamorous event on the calendar.

It used to begin on Victoria Station with the bright blue coaches of the *Train Bleu* waiting at the platform. Promptly at 11.00 am it would draw out of the station. Paris by evening. Dinner in a favourite restaurant, rejoin the train at the Gare du Nord, compartments transformed into bedrooms. The journey to Monte Carlo was not always sleep-inducing due to clanking noises associated with locomotive travel, but compensation was the first glimpse of Mediterranean blue as the winding track went through Cannes, Nice, Beaulieu-sur-Mer and finally reached Monte Carlo station, ablaze with geraniums, poppies and wisps of wisteria.

That experience cannot be repeated. The station has gone. Some years ago

Right: The picturesque harbour at Monte Carlo, where millionaires' yachts like floating palaces, jostled for moorings in race weeks.

Moira Shearer's daughter asked if I would show her where the station featured in the film *Red Shoes* in which her ballerina mother starred. Its significance is that although vulgarly extravagant, it was released at the peak of post-war austerity, and thus provided light relief and became one of Britain's best-loved films.

Scenic-wise Monte Carlo is much the same. Exotic ingredients are still there. Mountains soaring with jagged peaks, yellow ochre buildings on a succession of tiers, raffish architecture, feudal Palace crowning the Rock of Monaco, tropical trees and cacti the height of oaks in the formal gardens of Boulengia. The Romanesque Cathedral depends on Casino profits but is cynically dedicated to the Immaculate Conception. The floodlit Casino mirrors Charles Garnier's architectural design of the Paris Opera House, appropriate for operas specially composed for Monte Carlo by Saint-Saëns and Massenet, whilst Sergei Diaghilev made the Casino his base for the Ballet Russe de Monte Carlo. Even today's blasé visitors might react to the paintings on the ceiling of voluptuous naked women smoking cigars.

Right: Part of the glamour was provided by Prince Rainier, the lovely Princess Grace and their young family, reminders that this was the Grimaldi kingdom.

It is interesting to remember the scale of the Principality that lies in a Mediterranean amphitheatre. Only half the size of New York Central Park, yet it is self-contained with its own police, army, coinage, postage stamps, legal system, no income tax or death duties, and presided over by the Grimaldis since the twelfth century.

So much for scenery and trappings that the 'rookie' racing fan inherits, but not the glamour that surrounded the Grand Prix. The Gala Dinner used to be the event of the season on a par with the famous Red Cross Ball. It rivalled the yachting that was the focus of social life. Deep anchorage allowed large vessels to lie alongside the harbour. Agnelli had the *Agneta*, Sir Bernard and Lady Docker the *Shemara*, the *Creole* of Niarchos, the *Mahlane* of Sam Spiegel, and the *Christina* of Onassis. All that is now only a memory. Today the fan might inveigle an invitation from a tobacco sponsor to a promotion cocktail party on a hired yacht where nibbling and drinking help to shift one's brain into neutral as tongues idle on. After all, vulgarity is only the conduct of others.

The change coincided with the oil price rise of 1975. Arabs arrived *en masse*. The old set left in droves leaving the place to the *nouveaux*. The d'Azur began to attract visitors in baseball caps, lycra-clad toy boys, sweaty proles lying on beaches, slot machines, mobile phones galore, fast-food joints, pizza takeaways, Day-Glo hang-gliders. The Riviera has become honky-tonk.

Echoes of nostalgia can still be found in the Hotel de Paris. The resplendent Louis XV restaurant with flamboyant-style mirrors, where M. Froggier used to play his violin in between puffing an obnoxious pipe. The kitchen once presided over by M. Ducasse. The legendary bronze horse in the foyer with Louis XV astride. Generations of punters have left one leg gleaming gold through rubbing it for good luck before going to the Casino. The roof-grill where the Mediterranean can be savoured as your steak sizzles over a huge open fire. Sadly, the doorman who welcomed guests flourishing cap and flashing white teeth is no more.

In the halcyon days, the war of egos was fought on the green felt tables where baccarat and *chemin de fer* were the games to play, but the Gala Dinner was a night to remember, with David Niven linked with Grace Kelly before she became a Grimaldi, Callas and Onassis, Aga Khan accompanied by Dolores Guinness. No need to apologize for such vignettes. It is not name-dropping, just reminders of what used to be. BRM having won the Monaco Grand Prix five times left us many warm recollections. I think of Peter Sellers, so knowledgeable about every aspect of Formula One; Britt Ekland, sitting bemused in the pit area hating the noise; Françoise Hardy wearing a mini that made Britt's version look like a crinoline. Peter Townsend, whose help after the horrendous Bandini crash was so useful. I think of the reaction of King Peter of Yugoslavia and the Grand Duke Vladimir of Russia after accepting our invitation to watch pre-race preparations. The working garage was tucked away in a quiet side-street. To reach the first floor meant either walking up begrimed stone steps or using a creaking open lift. Such reality was not what our visitors expected. King Peter's comments became a mechanics byline. 'I had no idea such places existed in Monte Carlo'! After the initial shock, both men showed intelligent interest.

Right: The Gala Dinner at the Hotel de Paris was the event of the Season. Louis and Jean Stanley this year hosted a party that included Pedro Rodriguez and girlfriend Glenda, Ron Kass and Joan Collins, Raymond Mays, Ringo Starr and Maureen, Lulu and Denis Matthews.

Peter Ustinov introduced a light note in keeping with a man of mixed Russian, Spanish, German, Italian and Ethopian ancestry, fluent in six languages, and with a rare talent for mimicry. I recall Richard Starkey, otherwise Ringo Starr, and his then wife Maureen, joining us for lunch in the *Salle Empire*. The head waiter presented a special menu and recommended *langouste du cap à la parisienne* followed by *coquelet poêle des gourmets* and *pommes amardines*. Ringo's scouse request was peas and chips with a cup of tea, which I translated as *pomme frits, petits pois* and *thé citron*.

Monte Carlo attracts unusual characters. I recall Andy Warhol; film-director Polanski darting about the corridors like an under-sized bumble bee at large in a hothouse collecting facts for a documentary on Jackie Stewart in his long-hair days. I recall a guest sitting at a nearby table being the victim of a crude joke. The man in question had survived a nightmare experience when his plane crashed in an inaccessible region of the Arctic. To survive he had to resort to cannibalism

Left: Among the celebrities was Peter Townsend, enormously helpful at the time of the Bandini crash.

on his companion's corpse. Eventually rescued, the story became headline news. The waiter arrived bearing a silver salver which he lifted with a flourish. On the dish was a large raw bone with shreds of flesh. Such sick humour was like a man arriving at a fancy dress party dressed as a leper.

Alan Whicker came to the Monaco Grand Prix in search of topical items for a television programme. He told me he would like to sit-in at the GPDA pre-race meeting in our suite. Graham Hill was in the chair. He disliked delays, but waited for fifteen minutes. No sign of Whicker. His excuse afterwards was he had lost his

way from Nice. Hill's comment was typical. 'Anyone who can't find Monte Carlo from Nice should not be out on his own!'

Gloria Swanson's interest in the Grand Prix was unusual. Her sitting-room overlooked Casino Square. She said that whilst hating the thought of witnessing a major crash in which the driver was killed, she had a macabre wish to witness such a moment. Fascinated by the mystery of death, such thoughts haunted her in the small hours of the night. BRM won the race. Afterwards I said she must have been relieved that nothing dire had happened. Whilst agreeing, she added that the waking hours were foreboding. It was almost a premonition. Shortly afterwards, she died in New York. The time was 4.45 am.

I recall a pre-race lunch hosted by Walter Hayes. Fellow guests included Jackie and Helen Stewart, Elizabeth Taylor with boy friend in tow, and Cristina Ford. It was like a ringside seat at a feline contest of one-upmanship. Cristina overplayed her hand. Elizabeth held trump cards. When we visited the pits, everyone recognized Elizabeth, Cristina was ignored. Self-imposed silence was exercised when she said that as all the cars had Ford engines, winning was only a formality. Walter was left to correct diplomatically. Other personalities recalled include Jack Dunfee, one of the 'Bentley Boys', winner of long distance races like the 1929 'Double-12' with Woolf Barnato as co-driver; Bobby Sweeny, one-time British Amateur golf champion, who sprinkled huge chips like confetti on the roulette tables; Lord Soames' expansive grin, with Mary, Winston Churchill's favourite daughter; Randolph Churchill sitting hunched-up in the foyer, growling about the slow service; Prince Paul Metternich and Princess Tatiana, reminiscent of the days when gentlemen controlled the CSI; old-time 'greats' like René Dreyfus, Giuseppi Farina, Raymond Mays, Piero Taruffi, Count Lurani and Juan Manuel Fangio . . . vintage memories.

One final recollection. Among our guests was Joan Collins with her husband, Ron Kass. It was an educative experience. Joan's strategy with people is fascinating. She has the assurance of someone dealing herself a fifth ace in a card game with children. Nothing perturbs her, like having Cinzano poured down her cleavage. The only image she recognizes is the reflection in the looking-glass of immense dark eyes that widen to absorb everything, scarlet claws, high lip gloss. She is the original. For a woman of her age, her face and figure give hope to thousands of women.

By no stretch of imagination could I describe Joan as a motor-racing enthu-

Below: Nothing like optimism. Monagasque officials allowed Victorian-style park seats to remain on the Casino Square, with no Armco barriers. Spectators had straw bales as protection.

siast. That day she watched from the pits. The volume of sound almost had her screaming. Recovery was quick. The Gala Dinner coincided with her birthday, the chef agreed to bring in a birthday cake after the main course. To avoid over-crowding, one candle was lit, the cake duly cut with orchestral and vocal accompaniment, and a slice taken to David Niven sitting next to Princess Grace on the top table. Niven joined us later. He told Joan that Grace had warned him not to eat anything from that bitch, it would probably be poisoned. Afterwards both stars greeted each other with affectionate insincerity.

Today things are different. Princess Grace is dead. Instead we might see Caroline and Ernst-August and other members of the Grimaldi family, otherwise a sea of unrecognized faces. Such is the way of the modern world. What of the race? Monte Carlo has been described as a race of a thousand corners with as

Right: Joan Collins added the film star touch of elegance. There was no temptation to repeat the commercial advert of tipping a glass of Cinzano down her cleavage.

many as 20 gear changes a lap, or 2000 gear changes, one every five seconds. Today drivers are assisted by semi-automatic gear changes, pit-to-car radio, computer analysis of performances and obligatory pit stops - all very clinical, yet in many ways, in spite of obvious shortcomings, the old-style Monaco Grand Prix survived. It was unique.

Let us not forget that the first Monaco Grand Prix, in 1929, was won by a British driver, whose name appears in various record books as W. Williams or Grover Williams. His true name appears to have been William Grover, and he also won a Belgian Grand Prix. 'Williams' drove a Bugatti; another Bugatti, driven by E. Bouriano, finished second. Those were the marque's days of pomp, when Bugattis strove for mastery over the fabled P.2 Alfa-Romeos, which equipped Enzo Ferrari's Scuderia Ferrari racing team on its formation in 1929-30.

Left: Pits were an enclosed island round which the cars raced, whilst mechanics and engineers had to cope with basic facilities. Slim-lined Tony Rudd confers with chief-engineer Peter Berthow.

4
The Rodriguez Saga

Ricardo and Pedro Rodriguez were beyond cavil and question exciting figures in the 'seventies. Hungry for success, their determination to take the chequered flag never lessened. Enormous self-belief was fuelled by the encouragement of their wealthy father who was proud of his precocious offspring. At a time when other boys were worrying about school examinations, Ricardo was national bicycle champion at ten and motor-cycle champion three years later. Pedro owned a Porsche 1600 at fifteen. Ricardo had his Le Mans entry turned down by the A.C. de Quai because sixteen was considered too young. When both brothers graduated to motor-racing, success came in the United States of America and Europe with astonishing regularity, in spite of their being hard on machinery. Their personalities were different, no clones here, and found expression on the circuits. Ricardo more flamboyant, very extrovert; Pedro more restrained and introvert.

The Mexican Grand Prix of 1961 was a race of tragedy. Ricardo was anxious to impress fellow-countrymen. Ferrari having withdrawn from the race, Ricardo agreed to drive Rob Walker's Lotus 24-Climax, a competitive car with handling characteristics different from the Maranello car. Ricardo set the pace in practice, but with only ten minutes left of the final session, Surtees had taken pole position. Dom Rodriguez told his son to go out and beat the time. Hot-headed Ricardo needed no prompting. Maybe because the Lotus gave no sign of the breakaway point, he exited the banked corner before the pits at excessive speed, lost control and had a massive crash. Ricardo died of multiple injuries.

There was speculation about the cause. Broken wishbone and flat tyre headed the rumours. To get the record straight, I spoke to Rob after the 1998 British Grand Prix. His recollection was still clear. Scrutineers had made a thorough inspection. There was no mechanical failure, just human error. Driving before thousands of supporters, Ricardo had thrown caution to the winds. In many ways it matched Ronaldo's predicament in the 1998 soccer World Cup final against France. In spite of suffering an epileptic fit the night before, the weight of expectancy from 160 million fanatical Brazilians forced him to play. It was a mistake. France won the title. In Ricardo's case, it cost his life. At the funeral the President of Mexico articulated the country's grief in a eulogy for the 20-year-old driver.

Pedro's achievements were more impressive. In John Wyer's opinion he reigned supreme in sportscar racing. I regard Pedro's brilliant win in the 1970 Belgian Grand Prix as probably his greatest triumph. The powerful V12 engine in the new PI53 chassis made BRM a formidable challenger for the Formula One World Championship. The problem was the long-running controversy over the Francorchamps circuit. This gruelling test had claimed so many lives, that critics felt

Right: Ricardo Rodriguez, flamboyant and extroverted, lost his life by throwing caution to the winds by trying in front of his countrymen to take pole position from John Surtees.

enough was enough. The race should be switched to a safer venue. Pierre-Jean Stasse agreed that modifications should be made to ensure greater driver and spectator safety. Statistics proved the point, showing where the crashes occurred:

Archie Scott-Brown: Grand Prix of Spa, 1958 (near the clubhouse)
Chris Bristow: Grand Prix of Belgium, 1960. (Malmédy bend)
Alan Stacey: Grand Prix of Belgium, 1960. (Malmédy bend)
Spectator killed by Ickx's car: Coupes of Spa, 1964. (Masta)
Pietro Frescobaldi: 24-hours of Francorchamps, 1964. (Malmédy bend)
Tony Hegbourne: 500km of Spa, 1965. (Masta)
Karl Thielemann: Grand Prix, Formula V, 1967 (between Masta and Hollowel)
Eric de Keyn: 24-hours of Francorchamps, 1967 (Hollowel)
Wlm. Loos:, 24-hours of Francorchamps, 1967 (Hollowel)

With the exception of Scott-Brown, all the fatal accidents had occurred between Burneville and Stavelot. Clearly something had to be done. Promises were made, but little happened. Black spots were still Burneville corner, Malmédy bend, Masta and Hollowel. Anyone leaving the track at these points would crash into houses, walls, gullies or trees at speeds about 300 km/h. Only a miracle would save the driver. Part of the trouble was the organizers' claim that Francorchamps was the fastest circuit in the world. It was just that, but at a horrific cost. The GPDA held several meetings. Eventually the organizers agreed that in the event of rain various emergency plans would be activated. Should conditions become too bad, the race would be cancelled. The proposals were accepted by the GPDA. Race-day looked threatening with dark, lowering clouds and Ardennes mists shrouding the trees, but the rain held off. An incident-packed race ended with Bruce McLaren the surprise winner. Pedro was denied victory through the BRM P133 hiccupping through fuel shortage on the last lap and had to settle for second place.

Controversy continued the next season. Promises to the CSI and GPDA had not been carried out. Excuses were plentiful. The circuit was on public roads; changes were dependent on government permission and local authority financing; some municipal authorities were luke-warm about motor-racing. The inevitable happened. Ultimatum and panic-stations. I had a telephone call from Brussels. Pierre Ugeux was trawling for a compromise. Belgian delegation left for London. We met in the RAC Club. Three hours' discussion resulted in compromise suggestions which I took to a parallel meeting of constructors and entrants. The complicated plan appeared to satisfy doubts and fears about wet conditions. On race-day I was to act as co-ordinator between the Race Director, Mario Heron, Pierre Ugeux and the entrants and be in the control tower throughout the race. Everything was in the clear when insurmountable problems surfaced. Full insurance cover was refused. Had rain meant the race was postponed or cancelled, the BACB faced disastrous loss. The Grand Prix was not held.

Having learnt the folly of procrastination, the Belgians promised the safety measures would be implemented the following year. Optimism was misplaced. The 245-mile race was again threatened. GPDA inspection by Bonnier, Rindt, Stewart and myself confirmed that the work was uncompleted. To decide whether drivers would race on a rain-soaked track, Bruce McLaren tabled two motions. Members were asked if they would race on a dry track even if the safety work was unfinished. The motion was carried by two votes; similar motion if conditions

Right: Temperamentally Pedro was unlike his brother - more intense and introverted. On the circuits he had ice-cold concentration and ruthless determination. He was a potential World Champion.

were wet was defeated by the votes of McLaren, Hulme, Courage, de Adamitch, Miles, Servoz-Gavin, Beltoise, Graham Hill, Scarfiotti, Stewart, Surtees, Pescarolo, Amon, Rindt and Stommelen. Only one driver took the opposite view. He stated he had no hesitation about racing in the rain at Spa, or any other circuit. That man was Pedro Rodriguez.

His performance in the race was flawless. The combination of the powerful V12-engine in the PI53 chassis and Pedro's full-blooded driving produced a memorable victory disputed only by Amon. On lap 20 Pedro clocked a new lap record of 3:17.9. Three laps later the lead was down to three seconds. At the start of the last lap it was down to 1.7 seconds, but Pedro was still in front at La Source with the third car some minutes behind. After the race Pedro said he had only used 10,000 revs with plenty in reserve. With only two places at Francorchamps for overtaking, he was not worried about Amon's challenge. He did not think the New

Zealander had the guts to take the risk.

Pedro held strong views. He agreed with Denis Jenkinson's description of 'no-race-in-the-rain drivers as milk-and-water nancyboys'. Opinions that did not endear him to colleagues, but off the circuits, he became conformist. He felt the image of a racing driver should be smart and disliked long, untidy hair. The Mexican could have stepped out of *Guys and Dolls* with Runyonesque flair and deer-stalker hat, dark Latin appearance and enough charm to get away with anything. His hands were as voluble as his lips. He was not a good mixer with other drivers. It was deliberate. Getting to know people too well made it difficult to dislike them. When the chips are down, motor-racing is a tough sport. Favours are not given or expected. A telling tribute was the respect and affection he had from all the BRM mechanics and the workshop, and praise from team-manager, Tim Parnell. Of all our drivers, and we had many, Pedro received the largest fan-mail.

Away from the circuits Pedro loved parties and the social life. He was married to Angelina, a raven-haired Mexican. When he became part of the Grand Prix circus, he adapted to the European life, had a quiet set-up in Bray plus a blonde girlfriend Glenda. I am sure Pedro was equally fond of both women. It was a case of mares for courses. There were also extra-mural biological episodes so explicitly described by the tennis player, Guillermo Vilas: 'There are girls for one night, girls to live with, girls to take travelling. There are right girls for different moments. You can love a girl today, but maybe not tomorrow.' Pedro skirted round that advice, but was not always successful. One night in the Hotel de Paris at Monte Carlo, I was roused about 3.30 am by a telephone call. It was Pedro. He had chatted-up a young woman in the Casino who invited him to her flat, but proved more expensive than he expected. He hadn't enough money. Could I help? The obvious answer was to return to the hotel for more cash. That was impossible. She had hidden his clothes. I took the address and the amount, rang the concierge, who, used to emergencies, dispatched a porter on an errand of charity. The next morning at breakfast, Angelina complained that we worked her husband too hard. He had climbed into bed about 4.30 am thoroughly exhausted. I murmured I was not surprised.

Nocturnal interruptions of a different kind also occurred on another occasion in the same hotel. Pedro and Glenda occupied a room next to our suite. In the morning I told Pedro he would have to get the mattress springs oiled. I did not want to spend another night listening to the sound-effects of an X-film. Mercifully they changed their room.

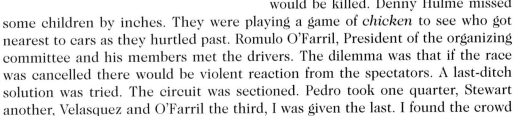

Left: Glenda, Pedro's blonde, petite girl friend.

Sometimes marital problems intruded on the circuit, like the day at Brands Hatch when the Rodriguez ménage arrived unexpectedly for a race. The sequel was worthy of a sit-com script. Dom Rodriguez, his attractive wife and the sultry Angelina were in one pit; next door Glenda sat with stop-watch and lap sheet. During the practice session, Pedro refused to stop at either. Instead the mechanics sprinted down the pit-lane when the BRM came in. The session ended without feline incident. Other vignettes recall Pedro's habit of suddenly producing a jar of tabasco sauce and hot peppers to sharpen the flavour of bland food: an altercation with a troublesome London taxi-driver that ended with the fiery Mexican spitting out the derogatory *peasant* to the bemused cabbie. There was also the traumatic 1970 Mexican Grand Prix. When we arrived, Mexico City was aflame with student riots and political demonstrations. Race organizers, fearful that the troubles might affect the Grand Prix, recruited an impressive task-force of army and police equipped with rifles, machine-guns and tear-gas canisters to patrol the circuit. Trouble came from a different source. Thousands turned up. Everyone wanted a front seat. Armco barriers were ignored. They climbed over and squatted on the circuit verge. Drivers were concerned that someone would be killed. Denny Hulme missed some children by inches. They were playing a game of *chicken* to see who got nearest to cars as they hurtled past. Romulo O'Farril, President of the organizing committee and his members met the drivers. The dilemma was that if the race was cancelled there would be violent reaction from the spectators. A last-ditch solution was tried. The circuit was sectioned. Pedro took one quarter, Stewart another, Velasquez and O'Farril the third, I was given the last. I found the crowd belligerent and abusive. They refused to budge. A hail of missiles was the answer. A journalist by me was hit on the head by a bottle. I spotted the fellow who had slung it, retrieved the missile, went over and suggested he had another go. The gesture appealed. The mood changed. Gradually the crowd was persuaded to get the right side of the Armco. Once the movement began, others followed suit. Eventually the race started. There were no further incidents until the penultimate lap when hundreds began to walk on the track heading for the pit-area. Drivers had to weave through human chicanes. Miraculously there were no casualties. When it was all over the Mexican organizers handed me a gold medal in appreciation for helping to avoid what might have been an ugly situation.

I come to the last few days of Pedro's life. BRM were in confident mood. The new P160 had proved its reliability and was tipped to win the British Grand Prix. Pedro was told to relax at the week-end in his home at Bray. The prospect did not appeal. Instead he negotiated a private deal to drive Herbert Muller's Ferrari 512M at the Norisring, a mediocre track around the stadium where the Nazis staged their rallies. This clapped-out car had been used for film work, but became competitive through Pedro's spirited driving. The car crashed on lap 12 of the first heat, ruptured a fuel tank. Pedro died in the flames. Our first intimation came from David Benson of the *Daily Express*. It was a tragedy that should never have happened. In Pedro's contract was a clause forbidding him to race in any other car without approval. That would never have been given.

Arrangements were made to fly to Mexico City for the funeral. There was the problem of Glenda. The situation called for extremely sensitive handling. I like both women. In the end we felt it had to be what Pedro would have wanted. We took Glenda with us. The Presidente Hotel had a private lift that went express to the sitting-room. Glenda was asked to stay put. If she went out, to do so from a lower floor, get off at the first floor to avoid the media and photographers. We went to the private chapel where Pedro's coffin rested in front of the altar. Throughout the night and the early hours of the morning, thousands of mourners filed past. We stood by the coffin for fifteen minutes, a vigil shared by the Mexican President. The road to the cemetery several miles away was lined six deep along the entire route by silent onlookers. Outside the chapel was a twenty-foot banner of red roses with the outline of Pedro's features traced in white roses. The cavalcade was absolutely unforgettable. Maybe it was mass emotion, but it was a genuine expression of grief. At the graveside I gave a personal eulogy. Then the police-escorted rush to the air-

Left: Pedro and Angelina at an Onyx reception in New York.

Right: Victory at Oulton Park with Alex Stokes, gear-box genius, in the background.

port where the New York flight had been delayed. From Heathrow we headed for Silverstone with a request from Pedro's family. The BRM he should have raced and probably won, would stand in front of the pits. We were asked to put a rose on the seat. It was early morning. No shops were open. A cottage by the roadside had a rosebush in bloom. I picked one, left some money and a note. It was placed in the car.

Much of what Pedro and Ricardo achieved has vanished through the sieve of memory. It would be true to say that neither feared death. Rob Walker recalled how before the last fatal lap in Mexico, Ricardo strapped himself in, then made the sign of the cross, the only time Rob had seen that happen. In Pedro's case, he was a fatalist. He once told me that when his time came, it was foretold. There would be no complaints.

I remember them as young men of real power, unafraid of the big occasion, with total dedication. Sadly we have lost their breed today. One personal memory is a letter written to us from Pedro's sister Conchita. This extract said it all: 'The comfort I have is that his work claimed his life, it was what he wanted and loved. I am sure that he lived more in the time that he had than most men who live many years longer. In the middle of my sorrow it is good to know that Pedro had such good friends like you who I am sure must have loved him. Thank you for all the trouble you went to for coming from so far away only to be with him until the last moment.'

5

Death in Berlin

On the paved 130 mph Avus banking at the northern extremity of the West Berlin circuit, Jean Behra crashed to his death. In the German Sportscar Grand Prix on a wet track. Having overtaken Jack Brabham on the long fast straight, the Porsche veered up the steep banking, hit a concrete post. Behra was hurled into the air, struck a flagpole, the impact snapping neck and spine. France had lost her greatest driver.

Jean Behra was unpredictable. On occasions I found him moody and tactless without being aware of doing so. Fear never entered his vocabulary. 'Egotism in an imbecile', said Sarah Bernhardt, 'is a vice; in an intelligent spirit, a virtue.' In Behra's case it was a form of self-encouragement, refusing to admit any man his superior at the wheel. Criticism was inevitable but tinged with admiration for the stocky Frenchman. Dissension was never far away. In 1959 he was No.1 driver for Ferrari with Phil Hill and Cliff Allison supporting. Ferrari took fiendish delight in unsettling his pilots. Tony Brooks came into the team. That meant the No.1 berth had two occupants. To make matters worse, Dan Gurney was hired. The unknown American set a pace as fast as Behra. Of the five Ferrari drivers, four spoke English, Behra was the odd one out. Matters came to a head at Rheims. Behra had a violent row with Tavoni, the team manager,

Right: Harry Schell (left) and Jean Behra - hot-tempered and impulsive both on and off the track.

and terminated his contract with Scuderia Ferrari. As early as Zandvoort, Behra told me he would like to rejoin BRM. He wanted to drive the spare BRM car at Avus instead of a modified Porsche. Unfortunately there was insufficient time to complete arrangements. His racing experience was vast. Like Nuvolari, Varzi and Rosemeyer, success came first on motor-cycles. On the red Moto Guzzi Behra won the Championship of France four years in succession. In 1951 he switched to four wheels. Amedée Gordini signed him to lead the Simca-Gordini team with Trintignant, Manzon and Simon. The gamble paid off in 1952. Ferrari were expected to win the French Grand Prix at Rheims with Alberto Ascari the favourite. Behra proved to be the surprise. From start to finish the little blue Gor-

dini set the pace. In 1955 Behra joined Maserati. The cars to beat were the Mercedes of Fangio and Moss. He won the Grands Prix of Pau and Bari plus the German 1,000 kms. In 1956 he was made No.2 after Moss joined the team, but this did not weaken his determination. Success tally was impressive, winning the Monthléry 1,000 Kilometres with Louis Rosier, repeated the German 1,000 Kilometres win with Moss; second in the Argentine Grand Prix; third in the Grands Prix of Great Britain, France, Monaco and Mendoza. In 1957 he was second at Buenos Aires; second in Argentine 1,000 Kilometres with Moss and Menditeguy; second to Fangio in Buenos Aires Trophy.

Behra joined BRM in 1957. It was a colourful experience. He won the Caen Grand Prix with ease; the International Trophy at Silverstone had its quota of incidents. Before the race he fell out with team mate, Harry Schell. Both men had fiery tempers. Language difficulties did not help. Trying to pacify them was hopeless. Behra was reduced to tears of rage. Even on the grid insults were exchanged as the cars were side by side. The finish of 1st, 2nd and 3rd calmed the situation. The other occasion was the Dutch Grand Prix at Zandvoort. Joakim Bonnier went into the lead with Behra second. The Swede drew away. Behra, unable to match the pace, became a mobile chichane. Neither Brabham nor Moss could overtake for several laps. BRM won their first World Championship race. Later Behra claimed a modest part of the celebrations. Another incident was at Goodwood. BRM brakes failed. He clouted the ridiculous brick chicane, wrecked the car but got away with severe bruising. He was not so fortunate when he crashed the Maserati at Dundrod. The lens of his spare goggles severed an ear. He had a plastic replacement. On occasions at dinner, he would cause a distraction by taking it off.

Over a ten year period, Jean Behra became something of a legend. In the same way that Graham Hill's helmet with the blue and white stripes of the London Rowing Club was instantly recognizable, I think of Behra's crash helmet with its chequered flag band and abbreviated peak.

Left: Banking at the Avus circuit. To cross the top white line meant trouble, as so many drivers found to their cost.

6
Italian Personalities

Apart from politics, Italy can claim a remarkable number of international figures like Pier Luigi Nervi, the architectural engineer; Fellini; Guilio Natta, winner of the Nobel Prize; Zeffirelli; Emilio Pucci; Raimondo D'Inzeo, Olympic show jumper; the Viscontis and so on. All stimulating and evocative. Two figures in Italian industry made a powerful impact in the world of the automobile and motor-racing.

Enzo Ferrari was a man apart. When he died in 1988, it was the end of an era. His long life covered the history of the internal combustion engine. He became the Grand Old Man of the racing car industry, a household name, yet few knew him. The isolation was deliberate. It acted as a shield. He was complex, at times insulting, emotional, devious, unpredictable, but could turn on the charm. My dealings with him went through all the moods. He used to say that it all began when aged 10 he was taken to the Bologna circuit by his father to watch Felice Nazzaro at the wheel of a racing car. The impact was like watching a space-rocket. The tough Italian won the race at the incredible speed of 60 mph. Enzo was next taken to the 1908 French Grand Prix at Dieppe, a formula libre event with no restriction on engine size, but the cars had to better a fuel average of 9.5-miles per gallon. In the race Nazzaro averaged 70.5 mph.

Enzo became an addict. The thrill of speed was to last over seventy years.

Enzo's father had a metal-working shop outside Modena, adapting axles for the railway industry. It was a steady job with modest returns. He

Above: Giovanni Agnelli (left) is to Italians what Rothschild means to France. A legend in industrial circles.

Above: Count Giovanni Lurani, who housed a fine collection of vintage racing cars in his castle home. On the walls in bold letters were the signatures of famous drivers.

was ambitious for his son, hopefully as an engineer. Enzo's first choice was an opera singer, but settled for a precarious career as a hopeful racing-driver. World War One intervened. Served in the Mountain Artillery. Duties involved shoeing pack mules, invalided out because of illness. Employment with Construzioni Meccaniche Nazionali gave him experience as a test driver. Introduction to motor racing came in 1919. He planned with his friend, Ugo Sivocci, to compete in the Targa Florio. To get to Sicily meant driving the racing car from Milan across Italy via the snow-covered Abruzzi Mountains, arriving at Palermo shortly before the start. The sequel was anti-climax. After a few miles a petrol tank fell off, repairs took time, then police caused further delay by halting all traffic entering the marketplace until a political rally ended. The car eventually finished the race but, by then, spectators and time-keepers had gone home.

Enzo's racing career had mixed fortunes, but lack of success did not deter. With the aid of Alfa engines and his own mechanics, a Ferrari team emerged in 1929. Results were better, but illness put a stop to active participation, hastened by the birth of his son, Dino in 1932. The Alfa period ended. The Ferrari era began. There were problems that never went away, highlighted when in 1962 Ford took charge of the sports-car division, whilst Enzo was responsible for the racing cars. Clash of temperaments soured working relationships. Enzo's autocratic style resented interference. He had little empathy with the Ford circus of

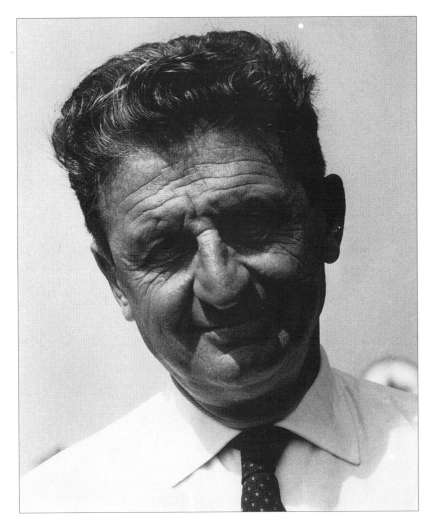

Above: Eusebio Dragoni had one of the most difficult jobs in racing as Ferrari team manager.

Above: Carlo Chiti (left) walking back to the pits after Phil Hill (centre) had won the World Championship at Monza.

lawyers, hatchet-men and financial advisers. When Fiat took over, tension lessened, but nothing was easy.

Enzo's outlook on life was affected by the death of his son Dino in 1956 of muscular dystrophy. It was a searing loss that left him even more isolated. His wife once told me over dinner that life with Enzo was made difficult by emotional traumas never seen in public. His dictatorial abrasiveness gave no hint of emotional upset over death. Involvement with actual Grands Prix saw him prominent with test sessions and qualifying tactics, but never seen on the important day. He watched the race on television with telephonic briefings to team managers. It was remote control. His dealings with drivers were manipulative, he liked to encourage jealousies. Two car entries with three drivers uncertain who was to be the odd man out. He argued that a happy team lost the edge of competitiveness. Enzo resisted the fashion of plastering the red cars with sponsor's logos and told me he thought it was a mistake to lose British racing green for livery of a cosmetic firm, however much they paid, but he had no qualms about letting Marlboro pay hefty retainers to his drivers, even allowing a modest shield on the cars

In his ninetieth year, Enzo looked frail, but still made his presence felt at Maranello, supervising the shop floor, wearing the inevitable dark glasses. His international stature was recognised when the Pope left Rome to visit him in Modena. It is interesting to recall an incident at Ravenna in 1923 after a race was won with Enzo at the wheel. During the excitement an elderly man gave him a piece of material that had been in a fire. It was a charred remnant of a scrap that belonged to the fighter ace, Francesco Baraccas, who shot down 35 planes in the war before losing his life in flames. The man was Baraccas' father. On it was a black prancing horse on a yellow background. Enzo's reaction was to adopt the symbol for his cars.

Before turning to the second most powerful figure in Italian automobile industry, a word about the influential designing flair of Pininfarina, uncle of Giuseppe Farina, the 1950 World Champion, the last of the old school with distinctive driving style, outstretched arms, head well back, and studying the track with a sideways glance. He was second to Nuvolari. Pininfarina had fame in a different way. Every car of his heyday owed something of its lines to him. He used to say that the Augusta was the first car with a sloping windshield. After that he put the radiator under the hood, then draped the body over the wheels. Every car owed something of its lines to him. His factory in Turin created the bodies for only fifty luxury cars a year until 1936. Then he began to produce in series, halted by the war, beginning again from scratch in 1945.

His reputation was enough. American Motors launched Pininfarina's Nash Ambassador with a 5 million-dollar advertising campaign in 1952. International

Below: Chinetti: distinguished driver who became one of Ferrari's most trusted engineers.

Below: Guglielmo 'Mimo' Dei of Centra-Sud.

recognition followed. He designed for Peugeot, Cadillac, and General Motors with four prototypes a year, in addition to designing bodies for Fiat, Alfa-Romeo, Lancia, Ferrari and luxury creations for clients like Prince Rainier and Onassis. His skills were global.

Giovanni Agnelli is to Italy what the name Rothschild means to France. An indefinable aura of mystery surrounds both. To the average Italian, Agnelli means Fiat which turns out 70 per cent of the cars on the roads of Italy. In industrial circles, he controls a number of corporations conservatively estimated about a hundred. He is the wealthiest man in Italy, made possible by the internal combustion engine. Ironically it made him an orphan when he was a boy. His father died in a plane crash, his mother in a car accident. Then in the 1950s he splintered his right leg in an accident. Many operations were required before he was mobile

Right: Romolo Tavoni (figure at rear), experienced disciplinarian in technical control of the Ferrari set-up.

again, but as a result he had to have an orthopaedic shoe on his right foot. Physically it left scars, but the disability was ignored. In his home a cupboard is a constant reminder. Rows and rows of shoes, but all for the left foot.

Agnelli's grandfather, Giovanni Agnelli (1866-1945), was a cavalry officer before founding the family fortune by presciently setting up a motor company in 1899. Its name became famous as an acronym: Fabbrica Italiana Automobili Torino – FIAT. He served in the Italian Senate, and during the Second World War, although then in his seventies, was made responsible for coordinating industrial contribution to the war effort. His grandson, born in 1921, was named for him.

The reason for the company's success and growth was due in part to the second Giovanni's ability to think for himself, unlike other industrialists who repeat contemporary clichés. In the Second World War he fought for Mussolini and Hitler on the Russian front and then with Rommel in North Africa. After the Armistice he fought with the Allied Fourth Army and was decorated for bravery. Realistic about adapting to changing circumstances, he likes space for liaisons of convenience. The names of Fiat and Agnelli are synonymous with Italy. The economist John Kenneth Galbraith rightly described him as unique among industrialists.

7

Feminine Trends

The Grand Prix circus consists of an exclusive peregrinating group of dedicated people. Everyone knows everyone, not necessarily friendly, at times bitchy, with an unspoken but accepted pecking-order. Motorhomes are prestigious bolt-holes. Superficial camaraderie extends to wives and drivers' girl friends. All nice and tidy, but falling short of what it used to be like. Maybe because the sport has become less gladiatorial.

Looking back over more than fifty years of motor-racing, the most noticeable difference is the lessening of tensions on race-days. There used to be worries that were never put into words. Such was the race casualty rate that the only reassuring thought was that if there had to be a bad crash it would be somebody else, a thought that sustained morale. In the meantime lap charts kept minds active.

If tragedy struck, as it so often did, there was spontaneous support and comfort. Reactions were so different. When I broke the news to Nina Rindt that her husband had died, she was calm, composed and tear-free. Her emotions were under control. Sally Courage was very distressed, clinging to the vain hope that if

Below: Amherst Villiers, engineer, scientist and artist, holds a captive audience.

Below: All lined up, pretty and pert, but nowhere to go.

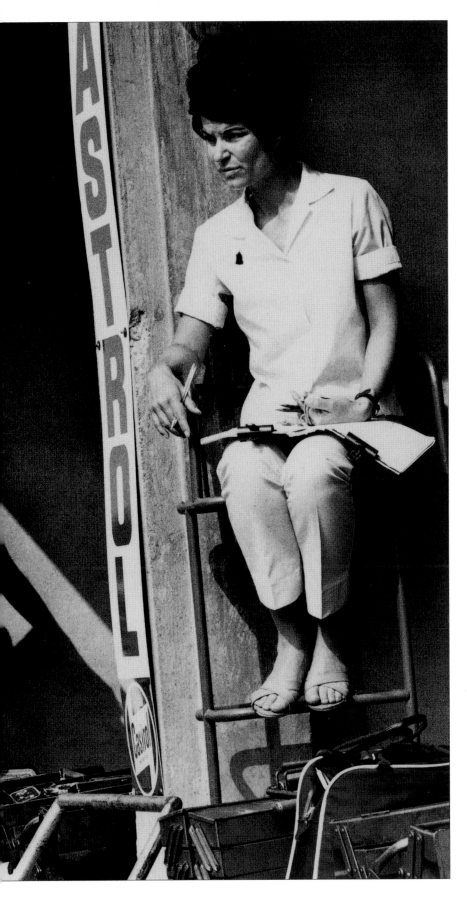

only Piers could be taken to the mobile hospital, all would be well. Her distress was increased by the insensitive attitude of the Dutch officials. Anne Schlesser was so hysterical that the French doctor had to be physically restrained from using a strait-jacket. On another occasion Pat Surtees experienced agonies of suspense when John crashed. I reassured her that no one had been seriously injured, but she could not stop shaking and was in far worse shape than her husband. I had to tell another girl that the driver she was living with had been killed. Immediate reaction was not grief but how to prevent insurance policies falling into the hands of his wife. I always felt that officialdom should have become more concerned and involved in the interests and well-being of the widows, most of whom were young with no financial resources or guarantees for the future. Instead they were forgotten. I know of many sad stories of acute depression, drug dependency, and alcoholism. Responsibilities do not end when a driver is killed.

Happily, safety campaigns have made these occasions rare, but divorce rates remain high, perhaps not surprising. Dewy-eyed visions of a glamorous life-style, endless travel to exotic countries, and unbroken sunshine are soon dispersed by reality of long airport waits, cheerless hotel rooms, living out of suitcases, climatic extremes, the realization of drawbacks being the wife of a selfish, self-centred fellow with diminished sense of responsibility and no identity outside a cockpit. Without helmets, they become anonymous off the track. Hardly heroic, certainly not romantic; divorce is a godsend. In this connection I think of Jackie Oliver. With his attractive fiancée, Lynn, they had dinner with us in Monte Carlo. They were planning arrangements for their impending marriage. Lynn wanted the ceremony to be free of any

Left: Pat Surtees, concentrated, but at times she felt the strain too much.

racing involvement. Jackie had other ideas. He suggested it should be immediately after the last practice for the British Grand Prix. Lynn was far from happy. She pointed out that their wedding-night would be interrupted by the bridegroom having to crawl out of bed at the crack of dawn to prepare for the race. Instead she suggested the day after the race. Oliver's answer was typical: "It would be too much of an anti-climax!" Needless to say, they are divorced.

Many drivers find it difficult to resist the attentions of female fans. Harry Schell was one such. His ambition was a girl at every circuit with the pay-off line "maybe see you at the next race." One girl took the invitation literally, turned up at Liverpool for the British Grand Prix, went up to his room in the Adelphi, knocked to say she was willing and able. Unfortunately he was already in bed with another wench. Without hesitation he excused himself on the grounds of not

Below: Sally Courage spots what Jean has seen.

Below: Paul Frère, veteran Belgian driver, with his attractive wife.

being well, gave her Jean Behra's number. The Frenchman duly obliged. As Harry said afterwards, it was team-work. Another wife of a highly-successful driver phoned just before midnight, to say she was going to divorce her Lothario. Two hours later she changed her mind. I pointed out that sharing her bed with a well-known driver did not mean she would continue to enjoy public recognition once the marriage had ended. I saw no virtue in throwing away a guaranteed meal-ticket and status. In such a dilemma, racing wives are second-rate citizens.

There were lighter moments. During race-days wives were gainfully occupied with stop-watches and lap charts, comfortably seated on pit counters, glamorized, unruffled, attracted by gawkers fascinated by their brief skirts who felt they had got to know the girl intimately. Such titillation is no longer possible with women relegated to ghetto-like enclosures, but I resent young upstarts who dis-

Below: Lynn Oliver and Colin Chapman; bookends without emotion - while husband Jackie prefers not to look.

miss women of previous decades as dull and uninteresting. On the contrary they were far prettier than the current bunch, as shown pictorially. All of them, young and old, were there to enjoy themselves.

A friend of mine, Teddy Tinling, asked if he could join us for the British Grand Prix at Silverstone. I agreed, but suspected an ulterior motive. There always was. He had the reputation of revolutionizing women's tennis gear and was famous for designing the gold-laced panties worn under a satin-trimmed jersey dress by the American 'Gorgeous' Gussie Moran. In the world of *haute couture*, no fewer than sixteen Wimbledon champions wore his creations, then he repeated the treatment by designing the uniform for the British Curtis Cup team. It was not successful. The girls were pretty enough but somehow the clubhouse convention had ossified the effort. It lacked the charismatic atmosphere of the Centre Court.

Tinling was publicity conscious. Over six foot tall, sun-tanned, completely bald, colourful clothes, earring in left ear, bracelets on wrist, he was noticeable in the pits. It was his first motor-race. Reactions were mixed. Highlight was the start with unbridled power released under control. He found it breath-taking, but thereafter it became dull and monotonous. Race positions were difficult to determine. Looking round he was appalled by the general lack of fashion awareness. It was just a mish-mash of trendy ideas. I pointed out that Silverstone was not a cat-walk. On the other hand there was logic behind his comments. He wanted racing women to become more fashion conscious, not going for outlandish creations decreed by Paris or Italy, though there was always a demand for bizarre creations as long as there were women who were peacocks in everything but beauty. He just wanted racing women to indulge in practical fashions of good taste. They were no different to other members of their sex. He said it would be safe to predict that women are never content with their personal appearance and always try to improve on nature, but it was dangerous to generalize. Dr. David Dickenson had

Above: A hopeful spectator.

Centre: Marianne Bonnier - expert time-keeper.

Above: Helen Stewart - just bored.

tried to establish the typical American girl by checking the measurements of 15,000 American women over a period of six years. The statistics were handed to a sculptor to produce a composite statue of the contemporary female. The result, compared with the Aphrodite of Cyrene, showed that the American women had a more masculine body, fuller hips and waist, with larger and more pointed breasts. Looking round the pit area, only one woman matched the description.

Tinling developed the argument that in normal feminine circles, women depend upon women for their dress-appeal. Fashionably dressed women are not interested in the appraisal of men. With microscopic carelessness their eyes are for ever upon other women. This drill is practised at the Grosvenor House in London when the British Racing Drivers Club hold their annual dinner attended by members and their partners. In all about 1000. Women are in their evening splendour, but you see feline evaluations being made of those whose appearance and dress fall below a self-appointed standard, and undisguised satisfaction when approval is won from women of like taste and outlook. In theory, women dress for men. In reality, women dress for women, and undress for men.

Today the ability to shock has become outmoded because every permutation of bad taste and sexual vulgarity has been tried, even to the extent of a well-known female designer announcing that she had shaved her pubic hair into a heart shape, a gimmick that would be wasted on a macho-type racing driver, who would probably be in too much of a hurry to notice. For several years a group of drivers' wives took refuge in a club called The Doghouse. Led by Bette Hill they enlivened the BRDC night with an impromptu cabaret to prove that the girls could rival the lads. Falling just short of a Full Monty display, no doubt influenced by a nudist club ruling that servants had to wear a small apron so as not to embarrass naked club members.

After all, motor-racing is meant to attract every type of female, including camp followers who, as Jack Straw might acknowledge, do serve a purpose!

8

Epic Races

It is not easy to short-list races of epic significance. The catalogue of success by drivers like Piquet, Prost, Mansell, Hunt, Hawthorn, Clark, Collins, Lauda, Villeneuve, Schumacher, and Hakkinen, forms a list that has become folk-lore. With such a profusion of richness, it has to be a personal choice. I have turned to less-publicised moments that were outstanding but now forgotten, drivers like

Giancarlo Baghetti who made his Formula One debut in the 1961 French Grand Prix at Rheims. In a field bristling with talent and competitive works-cars, the Italian was at the wheel of a privately funded Ferrari. After an exhausting race in grilling heat, Baghetti beat Dan Gurney by a tenth of a second. It was a superb performance never to be repeated. He died of cancer in 1995. Only a few remember.

PETER GETHIN

Peter Gethin had only one Grand Prix victory, but it made history. Monza – 1971. The 3.57-mile circuit set its usual challenge with high-speed curves and long flat-out straights, an examination that sorted out boys from men. That year we brought five BRMs. Jo Siffert, Peter Gethin and Howden Ganley were in the P160s with Mark 2 engines, Helmut Marko in a P153.

In practice Siffert had lapped 1min:23.95sec. Chris Amon took pole position, clocking 1min:22.40secs, with Jackie Ickx second. Ganley was on the second row thanks to a tow from Stewart and Peterson.

The start was sensational. Regazzoni was just ahead of Siffert as the pack hurtled into the Curve Grande where the circuit had been narrowed. As the race-pattern settled the lead continually changed until lap 14 when Siffert and Ickx dropped back, Stewart retired with a blown engine, the Ferraris were no longer

Left: The most exciting finish of any World Championship Grand Prix. Only 0.61 seconds separated the first four cars. Peter Gethin's record-breaking winning speed at the wheel of a BRM became and still is the fastest in Formula One World Championship. It was also BRM's second Championship victory in succession.

on the list. Amon had fallen back to sixth place after a nasty moment. Tearing off a visor-cover he had also lost his goggles.

Those opposed to overtaking manoeuvres might be reminded of that afternoon when the lead changed eight times. The field had settled into two groups. Gethin found himself in no-man's-land, isolated, without any hope of getting a tow. The only answer was to drive like hell. It worked. By lap 35 he was sixth, 5.6secs behind the leading bunch. By lap 40 the margin was cut to 4.9secs with ten laps remaining. The gap fell to 3.3secs. By then Gethin was with Peterson, Cevert, Hailwood and Ganley. Slip-streaming took him into the lead on laps 52 and 53. Confident that the BRM had sufficient power, Gethin dropped back on the penultimate lap. Everything depended on tactics at the Parabolica.

Cevert's ploy was to let Peterson through at the entrance, take a wider line and exit first to take the lead. Peterson aimed to lead through the Parabolica, banking on his acceleration having the edge on the Tyrrell. Gethin's challenge was discounted. So much for theory. Gethin, brakes locking, took the BRM on the inside line. Both cars were forced out wide in parallel slides. The BRM rev-limit was 10,500rpm. As Gethin told me afterwards, he had nothing to lose. In high second-gear, the engine went over 11,500 rpm. The engine did not blow up. Gethin won by 0.01 seconds. Only 0.61-seconds covered the first four cars. It was BRM's second World Championship victory in succession.

GRAHAM HILL AT NÜRBURGRING

Before 1962 Graham Hill had yet to earn a single championship point or even win a Formula One race. The V8 BRM marked a change of fortune. With the guidance of Tony Rudd and co-operation from Alan Challis and his mechanics, Graham had the car set-up to his liking, even though at times the tweaks seemed trivial. Nevertheless they did the trick. Goodwood produced a win at the Easter Meeting; then the sensational result at Silverstone in the International Trophy. The weather that day was cold and wet. The circuit was hazardous but did not deter Jim Clark. By lap 40 the Lotus led by 12.8 seconds. With only two laps left, the result looked certain even though Graham had reduced the margin to nine sec-

Left: Winning trophies included the Italian Cup and the magnificent Bandini Trophy.

onds. BRM road holding on a rain soaked circuit was put to the test. Driving to the limit Graham came into Woodcote Corner side-by-side with Clark, overtook on the outside and claimed the chequered flap by inches.

That victory set the pattern for the season. The Dutch Grand Prix was Graham's first World Championship success; sixth place at Monaco; second at Watkins Glen. Victory in South Africa made him World Champion. I have left for special mention the German Grand Prix at Nürburgring, probably the most significant victory in his career.

Memories of that race are still clear. Practice sessions at the Ring never seemed long enough, particularly when there were mechanical troubles or the weather was foul. The latter was the case in 1962, but there were other distractions. Friday session was marred by a camera accident that could have cost the lives of Graham and Tony Maggs. A 16mm movie camera fixed on de Beaufort's 4-cylinder Porsche broke its mountings and fell on to the middle of the track where cars were circulating at their fastest. Graham was first on the scene. Unable to avoid the obstacle, the oil lines were fractured, he lost control, the BRM plunging into the trees at 150 mph. It was the moment every driver fears, the uncontrollable seconds that span the dividing line between life and death. All Graham could do was brace himself for the impact. Examining the wreckage afterwards it was

Left: Sensational result in the International Trophy in Silverstone. With two laps left, Clark led Hill by 12.8 seconds. On a rain soaked circuit Graham cut into the lead, took Woodcote Corner side-by-side. The BRM went past the Lotus on the outside to win by inches. Graham's first words to Jim Clark: 'Mustn't do that again...far too dangerous!'

unbelievable that anyone could have survived, yet Graham emerged unscathed apart from extensive bruising.

We arrived late at Loch Muhle, an inn in the mountains with terraced vineyards as a backcloth. Bette Hill greeted us with news of the crash. Not having anything to ease the bruised bones, she had improvised with bubble-foam. I found Graham submerged in the bath with only his head emerging from a mass of bubbles. Later, somewhat subdued, he came down for dinner. Tony Maggs had been just as fortunate. There were no marshals with warning flags. He hit the oil, spun into the undergrowth. Maggs was unhurt but the old 4-cylinder Cooper had to be resurrected.

Right: Throughout his racing career, there was complete empathy between Graham and Bette. She worried, but never gave any hint of anxiety so as not to upset his concentration.

Torrential rain ruled out any hope of improved times. Dan Gurney's 8 min: 47.2 seconds was fast enough for pole position ahead of Graham's 8 min: 50.2 seconds; Clark 8 min: 51.2 seconds and Surtees 8 min: 57.5 seconds. Race day was just as frightful. Grandstands and the Dunlop tower were obscured by the driving rain. Electronic scoreboard disappeared in the swirling mists; Schloss Nürburg hidden by dark clouds. The pit area was like a river, 50,000 spectators sat silent and drenched. Reports came through of land-slides along various parts of the track. Eventually the rain eased sufficiently for the drivers to make a reconnaissance lap. Fuel tanks were topped up. The grid formed. The commentator asked the crowd to stand in memory of Wolfgang von Trips. Baron Leo von Diergardt dropped the flag. The field surged away with the exception of Clark whose Lotus stalled. He had forgotten to switch on the fuel pump. By the time he was mobile, the leading cars were in the back straight. When the cars reappeared, Gurney's Porsche was in the lead, a fact that Herr Josef Strauss, West German Defence Minister, standing by us in the control tower, was quick to point out. Teutonic satisfaction lessened on lap three when a trio of cars went past in clouds of spray. At the North Curve behind the pits, the silver Porsche was overtaken by BRM with Surtees' Lola-Climax almost alongside. From that point, the Bourne car held the advantage. The margin between first and third cars was never more than five seconds. When the final lap began, Graham's lead over Surtees was 3.5 seconds, with Gurney 0.08 seconds behind. For over two and a half hours both cars were never out of the BRM mirrors, pressure was relentless, no one put a wheel wrong. Afterwards Graham said he spotted a patch of oil, eased, and in a flash Surtees and Gurney closed the gap. Lap after lap the electronic scoreboard registered race progress.

It was agony waiting for the trio to appear on the brow of the rise leading to the finish line. With relief at seeing the familiar helmet in front. It ranked as probably Graham Hill's finest victory after battling over every yard of the gruelling struggle. Grand Prix racing at its best.

On the question of racing in torrential rain, Germany's reaction on safety measures left much to be desired. This was shown in 1968 when the organizers took an irresponsible gamble that had it misfired could have had horrific consequences. Atrocious weather persisted during practice. Lack of visibility and incessant rain made the Ring impossible. The sessions were stopped, a decision endorsed by drivers and entrants. On race-day, conditions were even worse. Stretches of the circuit were under water. Just before the start I was informed by two officials that visibility was so bad the helicopter aid would not be available. Fifteen doctors would be on duty with the circuit split. Anyone injured in one sector would be treated in the G.P. Mobile

Hospital. The injured in the other half would be taken to Adenauer Hospital. Theoretically feasible, the plan did not take into account the danger of a slow-moving ambulance driving on a fog-bound circuit with cars racing blind in clouds of spray. The possibilities were horrendous. A crashed car would have been difficult to locate in fog. Fires could not be extinguished. Spectators who only saw vague shadows hurtling past in the fog were at risk. Police broadcasts urged them not to move forward. Miraculously no one was injured but the organizers were irresponsible. They knew about the tenth lap that the weather had even worsened. Rodriguez, Hulme and Rindt told me afterwards that the race should have been stopped. Instead the organizers had a hunch that all would be well. A few weeks later in Milan, I was told by Herr Schmidt that a technical communications hitch had delayed the decision to abort the race. So much for the good old days! On the credit side, the race produced a brilliant victory for Jackie Stewart.

Left: Like Jackie Ickx and Pedro Rodriguez, Jackie Stewart was superb in the rain.

JEAN-PIERRE BELTOISE

Jean-Pierre Beltoise is part of the tradition of motor-cycle racers like Tazio Nuvolari, Piero Taruffi, Jean Behra,

John Surtees and Mike Hailwood, who were tempted by the thrills of four-wheel racing. Beltoise graduated after winning eleven French national motor-cycling championships, collecting in the process many scars. In 1964 a crash in the Rheims 12-hour race left him with a limp and weakened left arm. In spite of these disabilities, I signed him for BRM.

Reactions at Bourne were somewhat muted. I understood the hesitation for the Frenchman had a reputation of being short-tempered and uncooperative. He would bring an odd sense of detachment to the racing scene, variable, at times unpredictable, not a loner, but no one could say he was extrovert. He had a self-analytical mind that could almost be heard working. Warts and all, Jean-Pierre was a personal choice, not necessarily meeting with approval, but essentially a vote of confidence.

This conviction came as a result of an unusual legal case that revealed

Right: The signing of Jean-Pierre Beltoise as a BRM driver was a vote of confidence that was completely confirmed in his classic win in the Monaco Grand Prix - again in foul conditions. It was three hours of faultless driving in clouds of spray.

another side of his nature. It involved an issue that affected every racing driver and entrant and still does. It began with him being involved in an accident that caused the death of Ignazio Giunti and spawned a train of political and legal problems. Beltoise was arrested and charged with negligent homicide, released on bail of £3,125 with the requirement that he would stand trial in the Argentine within two months. If found guilty, the sentence could be two years imprisonment.

On returning to Paris he learnt that the Italians were pressing for life suspension from motor-racing. French authorities agreed and asked Beltoise to surrender his licence and suspend himself until the case had been heard in the courts. Had he done so voluntarily, it could have been construed as an admission of guilt. The Argentinian judge would pass sentence on a man who had already pleaded guilty. I was not at the race but was invited to Paris by Beltoise and Matra to study the film taken by French television, showing the accident in detail and giving a comprehensive picture of the tragedy and events afterwards.

Beltoise ran out of fuel. The car stopped and became an obvious hazard to other cars. Instead of leaving the car to be dealt with by marshals, he attempted at considerable risk to push it to the right side of the track. The gradient was too steep. Instead he

moved it across to the left side without any incident, then tried to push it along the track. Drivers could see what was happening and went past. Yellow flags warned to slow down and no overtaking. Beltoise admitted it was his intention to refuel at the pits even though it would have meant crossing the track, but the move was never attempted. The car was pointed straight. Oncoming cars were exiting from a slow hairpin some 200 yards from where the crash occurred. The lap chart and official lap times showed that Giunti, instead of slowing down, had increased his speed. 1:54.23 became 1:52.0. Immediately before impact, a car went past on the left, followed by Mike Parkes and Giunti. The Englishman took the left side. Giunti slipstreaming, pulled out to the right. His Ferrari clipped the Matra, exploded in flames. Giunti was trapped and died.

Checking the visual evidence it was clear that whilst marshals showed the yellow flags, no attempt was made to manhandle the car off the track or restrain the Frenchman from pushing the Matra. It appeared that another driver, Rouveyran, succeeded in getting his car back to the pits just ahead of the crash. He was not disqualified, but actually classified officially.

Beltoise was guilty of technical infringement, but blame should have been shared. Argentinian race stewards were empowered to hold an immediate enquiry and pass judgement, with drivers given 24 hours if they wished to appeal. The situation became more complicated through the Italians seeking a vicious sentence, even a Papal censure. French authorities put the onus on Beltoise. The Argentinian club remained silent. Their law courts delayed judgement. I was disappointed that the Grand Prix Drivers Association did not support Beltoise. We had a meeting in South Africa when a feeble protest was tabled. The fact that the issue affected every member was ignored. Racing in Italy and the Argentine posed such legal hazards that both races might be removed from the fixture-list. At a press conference in London I pointed out that this grey area might involve entrants and drivers. So much depended on the law of the land when an accident happens. The CSI was urged to safeguard Beltoise's interests at the trial. I offered to attend with the Frenchman if that happened. In the end commonsense prevailed. The heat was taken out of the controversy. Beltoise was assured he could race again in the Argentine. By that time he had signed for BRM. Sceptical about Argentinian lawyers, I took advice from the Foreign Office and the British Embassy in Buenos Aires. I withdrew him from the Argentinian Grand Prix and substituted Peter Gethin.

Beltoise' stay with BRM was enlivened by his dry Gallic humour, exemplary behaviour and support given by his wife, Jacqueline. It all came good in the 1972 Monaco Grand Prix, a race that almost didn't happen. After weeks of argument, entrants got their way. 25 cars had to be on the grid, otherwise the race was off. Agreement had been reached by telegram. Then just before practice began, the CSI issued a statement that only 20 cars could race. Drivers refused to practice. Police impounded all the cars in the underground garage on the seafront. Eventually the impasse was broken. It was a 25-car grid.

The weather on raceday was diabolical. Torrential rain made the roads treacherous. Beltoise, on the inside of the second row, had a superb start and took the lead as cars braked for St. Devote. During three hours of faultless driving in horrendous weather, Beltoise never lost the lead. Only one car finished on the same lap. Such was the Frenchman's determination that Ronnie Peterson told me afterwards how Beltoise, exasperated at being balked, stuck the BRM nose under Peterson's car and for several yards the Swede was driving with only the front

Right: Jean-Pierre Beltoise in the Marlboro-BRM colours.

wheels on the track. The ploy worked, Beltoise went past leaving a wall of spray, carving his way through the traffic with zero visibility. It was Jean-Pierre's first and only Grand Prix win but it was a memorable confirmation of our initial confidence.

BARON HUSCHKE VON HANSTEIN

Baron Huschke von Hanstein had an excellent record in competitive motor-racing and enjoyed the cut-and-thrust duels at every level of the sport. His ego was very secure. Firm disciplinarian as might be expected from an officer with a distinguished record in the German army. He enjoyed life. I recall many happy occasions along with Prince Paul Metternich and Ferry Porsche.

In reminiscent mood Huschke once picked out the 1940 Mille Miglia as his most satisfying victory. Everything about it was different, almost unreal. World War II had been declared. Close friends had been made enemies overnight. Italy was still neutral, but highly sensitive about the wisdom of the Mille Miglia being held, and insisted that the traditional route of this classic be switched to a triangular lay-out from Brescia to Cremona then Mantua and back, using normal roads, instead of the route from Brescia to Rome and back. The lap distance would be fractionally over 100 miles, covered nine times.

Inevitably national prestige was much in evidence. The BMW team consisted of six German drivers. After various permutations Huschke was paired with Walter Baumer, a young Mercedes-Benz factory driver. The open roadster developed some 120 hp against a powerful opposition, the main threat coming from eleven 2.6-litre Alfa-Romeos and two French 2-

litre Delage cars with such experienced drivers as Farina, Pintacuda, Sanesi, Biondetti, Comotti and Count Trossi, whose skills have long been forgotten, but who were racing drivers of distinction.

The race began at 4.00 am with one-minute intervals. Huschke recalled that fog was a hazard on the first lap, particularly in the Po Delta region, but once the race pattern took shape, he enjoyed a 1min.21 seconds lead. The advantage was maintained until the first scheduled change of drivers after three laps, but the race-order was so close that Huschke was told to keep at the wheel and increase the margin. He did just that, though conditions were becoming more difficult through road surfaces breaking-up.

After six laps Huschke welcomed the second scheduled pit stop for fuel and oil, anticipating a breather. At this point, Alfred Neubauer, the formidable Mercedes-Benz racing director, exercised his authority. His reputation was legendary. Trilby hat at an angle, taut jowls, his presence was dominating, if not overwhelming. Anyone who laid down the law to Huschke was no push-over. Orders were emphatic. There was too much at stake to take risks. He would have to stay behind the wheel for the remainder of the race. 300 gruelling miles lay ahead. Huschke told how tension helped to retain concentration, but he felt sorry for his young co-driver who was anxious to justify the ride. Sitting there hour after hour had damped enthusiasm. At this point Huschke showed that a granite unemotional manner could be something of a screen. Twenty kms from the finish he let Baumer take his seat and cross the finishing-line to a tumultuous welcome. It was a proud moment for both men. Not only was it the first 2-litre BMW to gain overall victory in this epic race, it was the first German win since Rudi Caracciola. The 923-mile course had been covered in 8 hours, 54 minutes at an average speed of 106 mph and top speed of 125 mph. The name of Walter Baumer is on the roll of winners. Sadly, shortly afterwards he was killed in the war.

In another capacity Huschke was a tower of strength controlling the sport in the CSI. He refused to be ignored. In those days there was no fudging. Drivers were not allowed to get away with blatant misdemeanours just because they had box office appeal. If the sport was brought into disrepute through their actions, they were either suspended or had championship points deducted. The present slap on the wrist would have been dismissed as inadequate. Would that the spirit of Huschke von Hanstein be revived.

He led a full life, but one ambition was unfulfilled . . . to race in a Formula One-type car. It seemed possible when before World War II he signed a contract to drive for the Auto-Union team. It was not to be. A mechanic rolled their car down a precipice, Huschke crushed his right shoulder and was hospitalized for a year. He never recovered full mobility. The weakness precluded driving what then were rugged power-monsters. Maybe it was for the best. He often felt he could have bettered the performances of some of his Porsche drivers. It was never put to the test.

PIERO TARUFFI

Piero Taruffi had a long racing career of amazing versatility. It began in 1923. Three years later saw his first win on two wheels at the age of 19. In all he registered 22 wins out of 41 motor-cycle races, in the process establishing 38 world records including the Flying Kilometre at 274 kmp, the Standing Mile, the Standing Kilometre, and the One Hour in 1937 and 1939. At the wheel of a racing car

Piero had 44 wins in 136 races that included the Grand Prix of Berne in 1948, the 1951 Carrera Panamericana Mexico, the Grand Prix of Switzerland and the Ulster Trophy. 1954 the Targa Florio, the Tour of Sicily and again in 1955. The next year saw victory in the German 1,000 Kilometre Race sharing the wheel with Jean Behra, Stirling Moss and Harry Schell.

One classic race eluded him. Time and time again the jinx struck in the Mille Miglia. Twelve disappointments. At 57 friends said respectfully and wrongly that he was too old and should retire; wrongly for when age is combined with such natural skill and determination, anything seemed possible. Indestructibly surviving, Taruffi held the gate against the younger generation.

Deciding to make one last attempt, Taruffi turned to Enzo Ferrari, who offered him a works Ferrari, a 4-litre 335 Sport. The race developed into a needle clash with Wolfgang von Trips and Peter Collins. Stirling Moss had retired early with a broken brake pedal. In spite of transmission problems, Taruffi approached Piadena only 200 yards behind von Trips. The advantage had shrunk as they came out of the last bend crossing the line together. Taruffi thought the German had clinched the issue, but was thrilled at finishing the race after so many failures. He was overwhelmed when his wife, Isabella, told him he had won. He told me it was his most satisfying victory. Sadly, the joy was diminished an hour later when news came through that his team-mate de Portago and the co-driver had been killed approaching Brescia. A tyre burst on the 175 mph straight. The car left the road. Nine spectators died.

Right: After twelve disappointments, success came at last for Taruffi in the Mille Miglia. Aged 57 he said afterwards it was his most satisfying victory. He immediately retired as Enzo Ferrari had suggested and his wife, Isabella, hoped. He settled in Rome, where he was honoured with a Doctorate of Engineering.

It was Pedro's last race. He retired to Rome with his wife, Isabella, where he received a Doctorate of Engineering as befitted one of Italy's greatest drivers and outstanding technical expert.

Recalling some epic races, one more should be added. It was the strangest race ever held, organized by the *New York Times,* co-sponsored by the French newspaper, *Le Matin*. Encouraged by a race they held the previous year, 1907, from Peking to Paris, they planned an even more rigorous test from New York to Paris via Siberia, the race starting from Times Square, along the Hudson River, then west to the coast. The original intention was to drive the cars to Siberia via the ice-covered Bering Straits. There were second thoughts. It was felt to be too hazardous. Instead the cars were shipped by boat from San Francisco.

On February 12th, 1908 six cars began the gruelling race. Problems galore. The Thomas with a covered-wagon top was held up by snowdrifts and had to stop at Buffalo for servicing at the factory where it was built. Early retirements were the Sizaire and MotoBloc.

After Japan, the Protos, an Italian Zust, and the Thomas followed the Trans-Siberian Railroad to Moscow, eventually reaching the finishing-line in Paris on July 26th. The German car was four days ahead of the Thomas. Race-distance was 21,000 miles and the event lasted 26 weeks, an incredible feat by primitive cars on roads that were often little better than dust-tracks. Such a test of endurance cuts the Mille Miglia, first run in 1927, down to size – and makes current Grands Prix seem like mere sprints!

Right: Willie Southgate, veteran BRM mechanic, shares the undisguised joy of Jean and Louis Stanley after Pedro Rodriguez's superb win at Spa.

9
An Engineering Pioneer

After every World Championship the victor is rightly acclaimed, yet somehow the praise seems out of proportion compard to the muted congratulations accorded to the recipient of the Constructor's title, formal recognition that the car has to be in the equation. I regard the car as more important than the driver. The combined skills of the designers, engineers and technicians put the machine on the grid. Think of the years when the Williams car was all-conquering. Such was its superiority that any competent driver aided by cockpit innovations could have won. The driver was almost irrelevant, yet when the chequered flag dropped, he claimed all the credit as if victory was solely due to his endeavours, and, what is more, he believed it. Reality came the next season when, at the wheel of a less competitive car, he trailed behind in the pack. The test of a real champion is when he can coax an ailing car over the line.

The Constructor's title is itself something of a misnomer. Many entrants are glorified kit-merchants who assemble the car with someone else's engine, gearbox, etc, etc, then give it the team's name. It is beyond their skills and financial resources of their budget to create a competitive racing car from scratch, Ferrari and BRM were among the few who blazed this trail.

In this connection, Raymond Mays played a significant role in the formative years of pre-war British motor-racing. An expert hill-climb exponent with many

Left: Raymond Mays at the wheel of his 'dream car', the BRM V-16

successes at Shelsey Wash, where as long ago as 1923 he held the record. He also held the record for the Mountain Course, the Campbell circuit at Brooklands as well as Crystal Palace. His rivalry with Prince Bira is part of racing history. He exercised pivotal influence on the imaginative project that produced the BRM. In the 1930s Germany dominated the Grand Prix scene. Two men attempted to break the stranglehold of Auto-Union, Mercedes-Benz, Alfa-Romeo, Ferrari and Maserati. One was Raymond Mays, the other Peter Berthon.

Together they shared the design of the successful, supercharged 1 litre, six cylinder ERA series. In 1947, they became more ambitious, with dreams of building a British racing car with a two-stage supercharged engine producing 600-bhp – the ultimate driving machine. Like many pipe-dreams, the snag was finance. When it came to persuasive powers Mays was in a class of his own. Charisma did the trick. Backing came from firms like Lucas, Rubery Owen, Ferodo, Dunlop, Lodge, Girling and Hardy Spicer. The British Motor Research Trust was formed, a co-operative with the declared objective of building such a car.

Peter Berthon's designing and technical skills made him the man for the job. The public paid lip service to its theoretical appeal, but few knew what was entailed. The preliminary outline of the V-16 was a sophisticated exercise in engineering, a $1\frac{1}{2}$ litre, 135-degree, supercharged engine of intimidating complexity and tremendous possibilities. Its cylinders measured 49.53mm by 48.26mm bore and stroke. It had Rolls Royce-built two-stage centrifugal supercharging, twin o.h. camshafts, light alloy heads, wet cylinder liners, quadruple coil-and-distributor ignition, and a two-piece 10-bearing crankshaft geared to a half-speed output shaft below, taking the

Left: Not many people really knew Raymond Mays, but his determination to build a racing car capable of breaking the domination by Auto-Union, Mercedes-Benz, Alfa-Romeo, Ferrari and Maserati never weakened.

drive to a five-speed gearbox with ZF differential, mounted transversely in unit with a de Dion rear axle, oleopneumatic suspension, and so on.

The translation of such a complex design from paper into metal took time and enormous cost. Hardly surprising the project fell behind schedule. It was August, 1950 when the pale green car was declared ready to race in the BRDC International at Silverstone with Raymond Sommer at the wheel. Unfortunately, before its first appearance, a public relations exercise went terribly wrong. No one in their right senses should have boasted about theoretical performances, then compounded their foolishness by publishing a booklet entitled *BRM Ambassador for Britain: The Story of Britain's Greatest Racing Car*. It tempted fortune.

The Silverstone outing was the final straw. The BRM V-16 was left on the grid with drive-shaft failure. The fact that afterwards the King and Queen expressed sympathy made the set-back even more embarrassing. It was a bitter blow to Berthon and Mays, but both were resilient, particularly the latter who showed sterner resolve than his public image suggested. Not many people really knew Raymond Mays.

At Eastgate House in Bourne he would indulge himself in the luxury of nostalgia over a bottle of choice Burgundy. He was an elegant figure with the kind of manners that improved those of a guest beyond recognition, but there were occa-

Below: The designing and technical skills of Peter Berthon went into the creation of this car, which he hoped would be the ultimate driving machine

sional bouts of depression. Loneliness was his greatest fear, and the thought of old age, which he deliberately countered by adopting an ageless pose. The house mirrored its owner. Everything about it was fastidious and meticulous. One of his concerns was the well-being of his mother: frail, haughty, the perfect hostess. Mays was pernickety about food. In that respect he was a dead loss as a guest. The pleasure was in anticipation, the courses were picked over.

Two happy memories; one sad. On winning at Zandvoort, he broke down in tears at the back of the pit. After years of frustration, it was a heartfelt emotional reaction. The second was as host to the *Club Interna-*

Below: Wedding group of Ernest and Florence Owen. She supported him in every way during the pioneering years.

Above: Alfred Owen and his sister Jean.

Above: Ernest Owen, younger son of the founder of Rubery Owen.

tional des Anciens Pilotes de Grand Prix at Eastgate house. For a few hours such names as Juan Manuel Fangio, Louis Chiron, Baron de Graffenreid, Philippe Etancelin, Baron von Hanstein, Stirling Moss and Amherst Villiers were reunited with the V-16 in full volume.

The sad recollection was in Stamford hospital a few days before he died. In no way did he look an octogenarian. In elegant dressing gown, silver buckled slippers, he was animated about current affairs, commented that Jean had changed her hair style, and asked for motor-racing news. I enquired if there was anything he would like. He thought, then asked if I could get some watercress soup from Fortnum and Mason. The next day by special delivery some tins arrived. The nurse told me later that it was his last appreciated meal. Raymond Mays takes his place as one of the old school legends, a worthy member of the élite.

After the Silverstone fiasco internal friction followed. With hindsight it might have been anticipated. To seat men like Tony Vandervell, Bernard Scott, David Brown and Alfred Owen round a table and expect unanimous agreement on technicalities and policy was indeed optimistic. Each was certain he was right. Fire and water do not commingle. Financial disagreements resulted in the Company being put on the market. The Rubery Owen board agreed to take it over. Vandervell declined to co-operate and walked away in disgust stating that a Grand Prix could never be won by a committee. He did his own thing, built the Vanwall and took the chequered flag.

The Rubery Owen directors continued the V-16 project. Extensive alterations had to be made at Bourne as the engine characteristics needed specialized machine-tools and test-gear. There was another problem. The Grand Prix formula changed in 1953 with the result that recognized events were limited, but progress was encouraging. At Albi, Fangio won his heat, broke the lap record, but had to retire in the final with mechanical trouble; at Silverstone the car finished second in a Formula Libre race, then won the Woodcote Cup at Goodwood. Ken Whar-

Above: BRM group of Graham Hill, Tony Rudd, Jackie Stewart, head mechanic Cyril Aitkin and the racing mechanics.

Above: Tim Parnell (right), popular team manager.

ton also succeeded at Goodwood in the new, lighter V-16 with the shortened chassis Type 15, Mark II. Ron Flockhart had four wins in four races at Snetterton. Froilan Gonzalez was in his element. The car suited his aggressive handling as he beat Farina's 4.5-litre Ferrari at Goodwood. Reg Parnell of similar build and temperament coped with the V-16's enormous power with confidence. Sadly there was no point in further development. Reliability had come too late. The Formula was out of date. The car had become obsolete.

The next phase for BRM was all-important. Changing ownership was not a solution in itself. The objectives were the same, but sceptics questioned whether there was enough experience at the top level to get results. The criticism was fair.

The fluctuating performance-graph of BRM is better understood by recalling the early history of the Group – its strength and weaknesses. It began in the 'nineties when Ernest founded what eventually became the largest private engineering group of companies in Europe. At the start it was minuscule. Serving five years apprenticeship with a Liverpool engineering works, Ernest entered into a partnership with John Rubery who ran a small factory with his brother Tom in Darlaston. It consisted of a smith's shop, minus its roof that had been blown off in a storm. The template shop had a roof so low that men had to stoop to walk on the platform. Power was supplied by a vertical steam engine in an egg-shaped horizontal boiler about three feet in diameter, fortunately with a safety-valve.

The workforce was a handful of men. Ernest provided the finance, but progress was slow. After two years his investment had halved in value. Main specialities were light steel roof-work and bridges. Fortunes changed with the bicycle boom that led to an expanding demand for factory construction, orders that expanded as the motor-car industry began. As early as 1896 the Rubery Owen Company was awarded the Gold Medal at the Richmond Exhibition for one of the earliest methods of frame construction, preceded by constructions of steel tubes, like the cycle frames, followed by rolled steel channel sections.

It was progress with profit, but at the outset there were many headaches.
Cash-flow was a headache. At one stage the weekly wage bill was solved by the
help of his wife, Florence, in the same way that decades later a shortfall in Colin
Chapman's income was helped out by his fiancée, Hazel. The crisis was averted.

Ernest Owen, as a pioneer in the engineering industry, joined that rare
breed of men with vision and ambition. Talent-wise, he could have made his mark
in several directions. As an engineer, motor-racing in its infancy appealed. Going
through his papers after he died, Jean found a circular official badge for the 1908
French Grand Prix, a 477-mile race at Dieppe won by Christian Lautenschlager
in a 12.8-litre Mercedes. Clippings from a French newspaper showed the youth-
ful Ernest with officials congratulating the winner. By a coincidence another
young enthusiast at this race was Enzo Ferrari. Ernest's interest in motor-racing
ran parallel with other thriving engineering projects. Automobiles had immense
appeal. I came across a Minute in the Aberdovy Council records of how Ernest
Owen was the first man to enter the little North Wales town in an automobile, but
had to be preceded by a man with a red flag.

In 1929 Ernest was taken ill. Duodenal ulcer complications necessitated
surgery that failed. He died at the early age of 61. His three children, Alfred,
Ernest and Jean inherited the estate including the works, in equal thirds. The
eldest son, Alfred, automatically took over as chairman, a nominal appointment,
for not only was he a student at Emmanuel College, Cambridge, but his engineering experience was nil. Vocationally he was involved in evangelical activities,
an obvious candidate for ordination. Enforced career change, he had to learn
from Charles Partridge, his father's right-hand man who virtually took on the
responsibilities of policy and expansion. Ernest, the younger son, would have
been better equipped, being an engineering student at Loughborough College.

Not surprising Alfred found it tough going. Compensating for lack of technical know-how, he developed strong qualities in a role as chairman. Delegation

was his strong point. The BRM project appealed from the sidelines. After the takeover, the urge to get even with Vandervell was evident, but it was still on a par with farming from Whitehall. Theoretically motivated, down-to-earth participation was not his role. In fact over the years only twice did he go to a Grand Prix outside this country.

BRM affairs at one stage were so chaotic that an ultimatum was issued. Do better or else! Change of directive had to come. I would have liked to see Ernest take the reins, but ever-conscious of the family pecking-order, he declined. Instead I was invited to become Chairman and joint Managing Director with Jean. It worked. Some decisions were unpopular but one proposed by Jean was significant. She was adamant that Tony Rudd should become Chief Engineer. He was outstanding.

We welded together a dedicated team that included gearbox specialist, Alex Stokes; skilled engineers like Aubrey Woods and Peter Windsor-Smith; Stan Hope who controlled the Body Shop; Wally Wakefield who worked miracles in meeting impossible deadlines; Willie Southgate and Neville Rippen in the Test House at Fokingham; Glen Foreman's finishing touches in the Assembly Shop; Head-Mechanics like Alan Challis, Cyril Aitkin and Phil Aylett, and innumerable others who worked long hours to meet the needs of a series of famous drivers. Jean's role throughout was wholehearted. Never once did she miss a Board or Technical Meeting and was present at every Grand Prix year after year in every country, in

Top left: Drawing Office

Centre: Section of the Machine Shop

Top right: Assembly in the Build Shop.

Bottom left: The finishing touches of engineering craftsmanship.

Bottom right: The Test House at Fokingham.

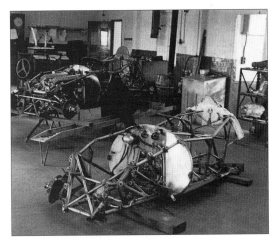

STARTING GRID OF SOME OF BRM DRIVERS

Juan Manuel Fangio	Froilan Gonzalez	Raymond Sommer
Peter Walker		Maurice Trintignant
Ken Wharton	Reg Parnell	Mike Hawthorn
Peter Collins		Ron Flockhart
Tony Brooks	Roy Salvadori	Jean Behra
Harry Schell		Joakim Bonnier
Stirling Moss	Richie Ginther	Dan Gurney
Jackie Stewart		Graham Hill
Peter Gethin	John Surtees	Howden Ganley
Pedro Rodriguez		Jo Siffert
Clay Regazzoni	Niki Lauda	Bobby Unser
Jean-Pierre Beltoise		Henri Pescarolo

Below: Highly competitive in the Yardley BRM livery.

Left: Fruits of success - Tony Rudd and Tony Brooks with Louis and Jean Stanley plus the South African Grand Prix trophy.

extremes of weather, yet somehow retained a feminine profile. When drivers were killed, and that was often, she was always at hand in a caring role.

In retrospect Jean and I had the satisfaction of knowing that every Grand Prix success enjoyed by BRM came during our stewardship. The record-sheet speaks for itself. Peter Gethin's record-breaking winning average of 151.31 mph at the wheel of a BRM became and still is the fastest in Formula One World Championship races.

B.R.M. VICTORIES INCLUDE

1950 Woodcote Cup, Goodwood	1st	
1950 Goodwood Trophy, Goodwood	1st	
1952 Goodwood Trophy	1st	
1952 National Trophy, Turnberry	1st	
1955 Chichester Cup, Goodwood	1st	
1957 Caen Grand Prix	1st	
1957 International Trophy, Silverstone	1st	
	2nd	
	3rd	
1959 Dutch Grand Prix, Zandvoort	1st	
1962 Dutch Grand Prix, Zandvoort	1st	
1962 German Grand Prix, Nürburgring	1st	
1962 Italian Grand Prix, Monza	1st	
	2nd	
1962 South African Grand Prix, E. London	1st	
1963 Monaco Grand Prix	1st	
1963 U.S.A. Grand Prix, Watkins Glen	1st	
	2nd	

1964 Monaco Grand Prix	1st
	2nd
1964 U.S.A. Grand Prix, Watkins Glen	1st
1965 Monaco Grand Prix	1st
1965 Italian Grand Prix, Monza	1st
	2nd
1965 U.S.A. Grand Prix, Watkins Glen	1st
1966 Monaco Grand Prix	1st
1970 Belgium Grand Prix, Francorchamps	1st
1971 Austrian Grand Prix, Zeltweg	1st
1971 Italian Grand Prix, Monza	1st
1972 Monaco Grand Prix	1st
1962 Formula One World Championship	
1962 Formula One Constructors Championship	
Tasman Championship	
Lady Wigram Trophy	
Ferodo Trophy	

Off the Record

Motor-racing, like any other activity in which the participants lay their lives on the line, is a serious business – and in these days, too often seems like just another offshoot of big business. But, although too many drivers today appear as glum, whingeing robots, it has had its share of humourists and eccentrics. The following candid camera shots aim to illustrate the sport's lighter side.

Left: It has been suggested that Don Quixote should become the patron saint of the FIA - they have so much in common!

Above: Jack Brabham at the wheel during a garden party at Belvedere Castle, former home of the Prince of Wales.

Left: Counter-attraction of speeds! At the German Grand Prix Red Arrows dive-bombed the circuit.

Above left: Very impressive – but I'll wager that his arms will give out after the first couple of laps!

Above right: I'm all right, Jack...unless that farmer decides to take back his milk churn and cream separator!

Top: In supporting races, grids could become cluttered.

Top left: Chubby figure of Charles Lytle, the American racing-historian.

Top right: Defensive stance by a spectator

Top centre: The good old days! For the first Austrian Grand Prix, an airfield was turned into a circuit by arranging straw bales

and an old London double-decker bus acted as H.Q. and timekeeping observatory plus familiar adverts.

Above and right : Brothers and Sisters, Let's forget the Immaculate Conception for a couple of hours!

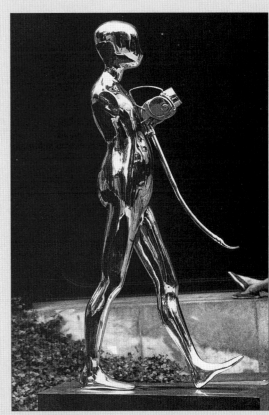

Above: Thoughtful service for the homesick driver!

Top left: The 'full' Dan.

Top centre: Gheti had a curious effect on Tavoni.

Top right: Recommended pit-crew uniform for the Millennium.

Above: The production Rover 200 BRM promises to be a good performer - 0-60 mph in 7.9 seconds.

10
Unacceptable Inefficiency

T he 8.76 miles Francorchamps Circuit at Spa set the ultimate test of machine reliability and driver skill. 1966 was no exception, including the Spa rain-hoodoo. Practice sessions were in sunshine, but the night before the race came thunder-storms and torrential rain, cleared by morning, only to cloud over half-an-hour before cars assembled on the grid. A news-flash announced in French over the loudspeaker that heavy rain was falling at Stavelot. English ears missed the point. The flag dropped. Surtees surged into the lead followed by Rindt and Stewart. The field disappeared out of sight. The P.A. announced exceptionally heavy rain at Malmédy. Usually the roar of approaching engines could be heard from Blanchimont. This time everything was quiet. One car appeared at La Source. It was Surtees. Ten seconds later Brabham and Bandini came through. Ginther, Rindt and Ligier followed at intervals. Then nothing. Only six cars had survived. Eventually the official announcement stated that the cars had struck a river of rainwater flowing across the tract after Burneville at speeds of some 140 mph. Bonnier had spun and clouted Spence. Siffert braking hard was hit by Hulme. Rindt spun in front of Brabham. Stewart, next to spin, went off the road. Bondurant finished upside down in a ditch. Graham Hill hit straw bales. Pushing the machine back on the track, he saw Stewart trapped in a

Right: Sombre moment on a sunny afternoon as an ambulance leaves the circuit carrying the body of a young driver. Shortly after another vehicle went past with another fatality. Crashes cost the lives of Alan Stacey and Chris Bristow.

wrecked BRM. He tried to free his team-mate, but he was trapped in the buckled chassis. Bondurant, badly shaken, crawled out of his damaged car and staggered across to help. Fortunately a spectator provided some tools. Stewart was released and carried to a nearby barn.

Twenty-five minutes passed before an ambulance arrived. When I arrived Stewart was still in shock with shoulder, hip and back injuries plus fuel burns. Instead of a helicopter, he was put in an ambulance. Police outriders did their best to clear the road, but progress was slow, bumpy and painful. Then the police escort disappeared and the ambulance driver lost his way. Hospital staff at Verviers were helpful, but lacked the facilities of a larger hospital. Jim Clark and

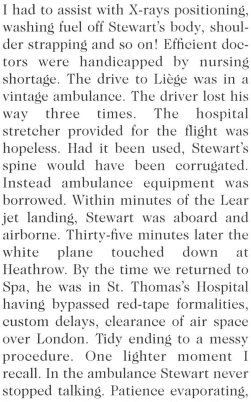

Right: Impressive mobile hospital of the International Grand Prix Medical Service.

I had to assist with X-rays positioning, washing fuel off Stewart's body, shoulder strapping and so on! Efficient doctors were handicapped by nursing shortage. The drive to Liège was in a vintage ambulance. The driver lost his way three times. The hospital stretcher provided for the flight was hopeless. Had it been used, Stewart's spine would have been corrugated. Instead ambulance equipment was borrowed. Within minutes of the Lear jet landing, Stewart was aboard and airborne. Thirty-five minutes later the white plane touched down at Heathrow. By the time we returned to Spa, he was in St. Thomas's Hospital having bypassed red-tape formalities, custom delays, clearance of air space over London. Tidy ending to a messy procedure. One lighter moment I recall. In the ambulance Stewart never stopped talking. Patience evaporating,

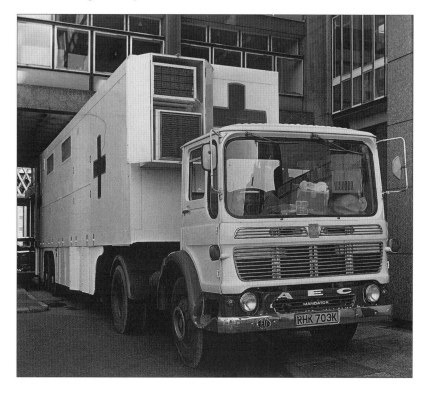

I stemmed the verbiage. 'Look Stewart, I don't mind you using my Christian name, but for God's sake pronounce it properly. It is Louis not *Lewis*'. Jackie has quoted that story many times. He said it jolted him out of shock!

The muddle surrounding the Stewart crash underlined the need for reform. It highlighted the inefficiency and indifference of officials to a flawed structure. An indirect result was the introduction of the International Grand Prix Medical Service in the form of a mobile hospital that went to all the European circuits staging Formula One World Championship races. It did not happen by chance. Detailed planning for design was all-important. I sought advice from specialists like General Stephen of the Ministry of Defence and Major John Iffland, an expert on the capabilities of field hospitals.

Equipment chosen simplified treatment, like the X-ray machine independent of external power supply operating off two 12-volt batteries with an automatic developing process. Working on the polaroid principle, dark-room facilities were not needed. Surgeons had the result in a matter of seconds. Hydraulic lifts eliminated dangerous tilting. Trolleys had X-ray lucent tops which avoided moving a patient. Electric respirators with electric suction apparatus. Air splints modified and approved by the Birmingham Accident Hospital. Blood bank with refrigerators and plasma substitutes. Blood idiosyncrasies were anticipated. Air-lock doors kept the atmosphere clean. Ventilation and temperature levels were controlled by positive pressure. Air-conditioning throughout. Humidity 65° and temperature 75°. Treatment of burns was given special attention by military experts. A new form of treatment was developed by a research team of London specialists and approved by Burns Centres.

I was not forgetful that an injured person might not be a driver. It could have been a marshal, mechanic, trade representative, journalist or photographer – all exposed to the hazards of motor-racing. Simple questionnaires were circulated that gave the doctor relevant medical history such as blood group, tetanus immunization, previous cortisone therapy, stimulants or sedatives, allergy and sensitivity to pain-killing drugs, morphine, pethidine, antibiotics, iodine, elastoplast and so on. Also listed were previous serious illnesses, operations, anaesthetics and complications.

Right: Corner of the clinical interior. James Purrell, theatre technician, whose services were invaluable.

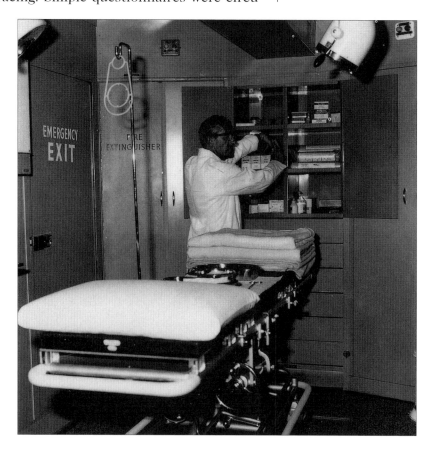

The Mobile Hospital came up to expectations on design, equipment and capability. It featured in four Medical Conferences, shown on *Tomorrow's World* by Raymond Baxter, and welcomed by the President of Ghana as the role model for the inauguration of a National Health Service in his country. In many ways it was unique.

The next step was to establish a working procedure acceptable to the motor-racing scene. I felt it was necessary for each country to have its own Advisory Council. Gradually the montage took shape.

Germany was represented by Prince Paul von Metternich, President of Automobilclubs von Deutschland; Baron von Diergardt, Avus-Sportpresident; Baron Huschke von Hanstein; Herbert Schmidt and Dr. Eduard Rothenhelder.

Holland by Jonkheer Andringa de Kempenaar, President R.N.A.C.; Jr. J. Kniphorst, Vice-President R.N.A.C.; John Hugenholtz, Director of Zandvoort Circuit; John Corsmit, Director of Sporting Division; Dr. Fokke Bosch, Head of the Medical Committee; Dr. W. Steensma and Dr. Zwarey.

France had Jacques Finance, President of F.F.S.A. (representing the A.C.O. and President of the French Federation); Jean Savale, President of A.S.A.C. Basco-Bearnais; Jean Lucas, A.S. of the A.C.R.P (representing the Trophe de France at Monthléry): Raymond Roche, Secretary-General of A.C. Champagne; M. Brouzes, President of Auto Moto Camping Club and E.G.J. Crombac.

Monaco had Antony Noghes, President-Fondateur of A.C. of Monaco; Claude Fin, Commissaire General Adjoint; Jacques Taffe, Commissaire-General; Louis Chiron, Director of the Course.

Belgium had Prince Amaury de Merode, President of R.A.C. of Belgium; Hubert de Harlez, Secretary of Commission Sportive Nationale; Pierre-Jean Stasse, Member of Commission Sportive Nationale.

Italy had Ing. P. Campanella, President of Competition Committee of A.C. of Italy;Count Giovanni Lurani, Vice-President of A.C. of Milan and Vice-President of S.I.A.S. (Monza); Comm. Gigi Villoresi, Member of Council of A.C. of Milan; Ing. G. Bacciagaluppi, Secretary-General of Italian Competition Committee and Director of Monza Circuit.

Left: Inauguration of the Medical Service took place at Oulton Park. It was dedicated by the Bishop of Chester, Lord Chesham formally handing me the keys as Director-General.

United States of America: Cameron Argetsinger, Executive-Director of Watkins Glen G.P. Corporation; Wiliam Milliken, Director of Watkins G.P. Corporation; Dr. Francis Ward, Director of Medical Staff; Dr. Frank Falkner, University of Louisville Medical School.

Great Britain by Jack Brabham, plus nominated officials and medical team for each circuit. *Medical Advisory Panel* headed by Sir Reginald Watson-Jones; Major-General R.A. Stephen, Director of Surgery, Ministry of Defence; Major John Iffland and Brian Truscott, Consultant Surgeon to United Cambridge Hospitals. *General Advisory Panel* consisted of Maurice Baumgartner, president of Commission Sportive International and Joakim Bonnier, President of Grand Prix Drivers Association.

Setting up these national advisory councils was time-consuming but response justified the effort. The inauguration of the International Grand Prix Medical Service took place at Oulton Park when the Mobile Hospital was dedicated by the Bishop of Chester and the keys formally handed to me as Director-General by Lord Chesham.

One headache remained. Once the unit went into action there was no guarantee that the doctors on duty would be first-class. Past experience had shown time and again that standards fluctuated alarmingly. The medical profession is sensitive when it comes to criticism, on a par with accusing the Vatican of immorality, but even the most touchy would have condemned some of their colleagues. I think of a driver in considerable pain from a smashed cheek-bone. Asking why a pain-reliever had not been given, I was told by the surgeon that anaesthetics were not necessary. Once on the operating table the pain would put him out. I recall a driver complaining that the doctor who treated him at Brands Hatch smelt strongly of alcohol. Another medico at the same circuit was rebuked for treating a wound with filthy finger-nails. Monza had unacceptable standards. The first-aid post at the circuit reeked of tobacco fumes, littered with empty beer cans, spittoons would have been useful. This was where a driver suffering from burns would have been initially treated. Stewart once needed treatment for burns. The pit surgery was locked. No one knew where the doctor had gone. Eventually located watching above the pits, opened up, dropped a scalpel in the dust, wiped it on the back of his jacket and used it without hesitation. The list could be extended but these instances suffice.

The choice was limited. Top doctors and surgeons were too busy to bother with self-inflicted injuries. It had to be second-best. Student doctors with limited

experience; enthusiasts who anticipated free days racing with hopefully no one needing professional attention; oldies past their sell-by date but conscious of brassard status and perks. That was where the National Advisory Committees helped. It was certainly not the job of a layman. On the whole it worked, but there were set-backs. A few instances show what it used to be like. The good old days did not always live up to their name. A fresh generation has no idea what sometimes happened.

Take the treatment of Bob Anderson, a private entrant with great potential. In an outclassed car he gained World Championship points, including victories in the Rome Grand Prix and Rhodesian Grand Prix, 3rd in Imola, 4th in Syracuse, 3rd in the Austrian Grand Prix and 5th in South Africa. In more powerful, reliable machinery it would have been a different story. As it was he had high hopes for the Canadian Grand Prix. On the eve of his departure he crashed testing his Formula One Brabham-Climax at Silverstone. He was trapped in his car for half-an-hour before medical aid arrived. The usual doctor was away and no one knew where to find the locum. Several people, including the BRDC President Gerald Lascelles, did everything possible to locate a medic. All this time Anderson was in terrible pain. The force of impact left both lungs perforated against the steering-wheel. Eventually he was lifted from the car and transferred to what Silverstone described as an ambulance. The vehicle, second-hand, had poor springs, no equipment other than a stretcher, and a dirty floor. Alan Brodie, his mechanic, was with Anderson throughout and recorded what happened. The driver's condition worsened. There was no oxygen and nobody with medical knowledge. There was no way to ease the pain, made worse by the poor springing and uneven road surface. Heavy traffic made progress slow. Brodie asked the driver to sound the

Left: Bob Anderson, talented young driver, who died in agony after crashing in a practice session at Silverstone. Confusion over the circuit's emergencies systems caused the distress.

bell or siren. The ambulance had neither. The Northampton ambulance met them before they reached the hospital. Anderson was too ill to be transferred. Oxygen equipment was put in the Silverstone vehicle. Shortly after arrival at the hospital Bob Anderson died.

Silverstone at that time had defects. Nominal charge was made for practice on the circuit, but no one was officially present with medical or first-aid experience, the first-aid post was closed and locked. There were two 'ambulance-type' vehicles with a man available to drive to Northampton Hospital. In the event of a crash during testing, there was always the possibility of fire. The employee who might drive the ambulance was also responsible for handling a fire-fighting vehicle. Every season members of the Grand Prix Drivers Association were asked to assess on a 1-10 marking the medical and safety facilities at every World Championship circuit. Silverstone ranked next to last, just ahead of Mexico. Those who

Right: Jochen Rindt, another driver whose death was aggravated by Italian red tape. Nationalistic bias was partly to blame.

attended the Silverstone Golden Jubilee Raceday in October 1998 were impressed by the facilities and the scale of proposed future plans. They appear to fall short of the standards required by Bernie Ecclestone.

Continental circuits had fluctuating standards. When Jochen Rindt crashed at Monza he was lifted from the wrecked Lotus with multiple injuries. Chapman and Stewart alerted the Mobile Hospital. Everything was ready, lift lowered for the stretcher. Surgeon, anaesthetist, nurses and theatre technician were waiting. The ambulance came to a halt beside the hospital. Ignoring the lift, Rindt was transferred to another ambulance. I asked why the hospital facilities were ignored. No reason was given. Chapman asked if I would go with Rindt. The slow journey to Milan took over an hour. A medical attendant did all he could. I was asked to hold the drip. When we reached the hospital gates, Rindt died. I returned to Monza. At a press conference I criticized the Italian officials for ignoring the Mobile Hospital; maybe the driver's life could not have been saved, but he would have died without pain and his wife by his side. The next day as the cars assembled on the grid, I was approached by two Italians who told me that unless I retracted the criticism made to the press, my passport would be seized. I suggested in basic English where they could go. When the race finished, nothing happened. The next morning at a meeting in the Automobile Club in Milan attended by FIA delegates and CSI, an Italian official asked me to sign a prepared statement to the effect that a Professor of Medicine was also in the ambulance. I declined.

The attitude by Silverstone officials was at times negative. Several days before the British Grand Prix, I approached Dean Delamont to find out where the Mobile Hospital was to be sited. He indicated the place which was first-class, more or less out of public sight, with immediate access from the circuit and a clear run for an ambulance to draw up in front of the lift. A patient could have been transferred in seconds into the resuscitation section. Arriving at the circuit on race day, I found the hospital had been moved to an unacceptable site on rough ground with no privacy. Every car that passed would have sent up clouds of dust. It was so close to a trade caravan that an ambulance could not pull in, whilst the lift could only be operated with difficulty. Had an accident occurred which necessitated immediate specialized medical or surgical attention, the delay and difficulty of getting an injured man into the hospital could have been serious. The person responsible for shifting the hospital was an official whose remarks in front of witnesses summed it up. 'We've never had this type of hospital before. If a man gets injured, he'll just have to take his chance like anybody else. I don't believe in molly-coddling any driver.' Protests to the President and Committee members produced a satisfactory solution. In future the Mobile Hospital was placed alongside the existing first-aid post with doctors, nurses and permanent staff working as a team.

Right: Light-hearted gesture by Walter Hayes.

At times doctors are reluctant to co-operate. Graham Hill crashed in the 1970 American Grand Prix at Watkins Glen with 18 laps to go. On the previous lap it was noticed that the left rear tyre was deflating. Prior to this Graham had spun on some oil and gone on the grass. He undid the safety harness, checked if the car was alright, and as the car would not fire, pushed it on a downhill slope, jumped in and restarted, but could not fasten the belts. As he went past the pits, Hill indicated the suspect tyre but did not complete the lap. The tyre lost its air, the car went off the track and overturned at high speed. Hill was thrown out with serious injuries to both legs and taken to Elmira Hospital. As he was being wheeled into the operating theatre, Graham, retaining his sense of humour, asked me to phone Bette and say it was unlikely that he could go to a party planned in a few days' time. The doctors were anxious to tackle a delicate operation affecting both legs. Unfortunately the main surgeon was in Washington. Reluctantly they contacted him on the telephone and described the extent of the injuries. The specialist advised immediate action on one leg, but the other leg was different. Facilities and treatment at St. Thomas's Hospital in London would be better, provided the journey was taken as quickly as possible. Medical protocol could be rigid. When Lorenzo Bandini crashed in Monaco and sustained terrible burns, a cross-section of officials, relatives, Ferrari manager, Dean Delamont, Lord Camden and CSI members met in my room in the Hotel de Paris. The implications of the crash were discussed. It was felt that a burns specialist from East Grinstead should be flown over. Although past midnight, the hospital agreed that specialists

For Louis Stanley –
"The Florence Nightingale of Motor Racing.
– but seriously, as a small salute to the Grand Prix Medical Service.

Walter Hayes.

could leave immediately but the proposal did not meet with the approval of the Monagasque doctors. They objected to interference by an English specialist. Second opinions were not always welcome. In Bandini's case, his injuries and burns were too grave for medical aid. In one sense it was merciful that he passed away.

Looking back, I wondered at times whether all the work involved in setting-up the Grand Prix Medical Service was worthwhile. It was prompted by the horror of seeing so many friends injured, disfigured and killed. Witnessing violent deaths leaves scars. I shall never forget seeing Jo Siffert slumped over the wheel, burnt to death due to the inefficient fire-fighting service at Brands Hatch. Roger Williamson's fatal crash at Zandvoort when his car went into an Armco barrier and became engulfed in flames from ruptured fuel lines. Tom Wheatcroft, grief-stricken, asked if I would go with him to the mortuary for identification formalities. The mortuary attendant gave me the key to unscrew one side of the coffin. The lid was raised. Seeing Roger still in flame-scarred clothes was a memory that has never gone. The same applied to Jo Schlesser's crash at Rouen when his blackened body was brought to the hospital. I think of other drivers who died not from injuries, but from infections caught in foreign hospitals. Such needless loss of life made motor-racing seem futile.

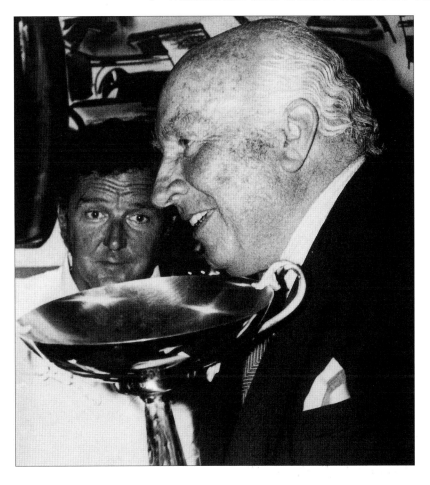

Left: Louis Stanley receiving a trophy from the Austrian officials as a tribute to the services given by the IGPMS.

Reactions such as these motivated the creation of the Medical Service. The project cost Jean and I thousands of pounds. It was an attempt to bring something positive to a potentially lethal sport. We wanted nothing in return. The fact that lives had been saved and suffering alleviated was reward enough. The policy we adopted of refusing press interviews and media publicity was possibly a disadvantage, but we felt that medical treatment should be a private affair. It was gratifying to receive so many letters of appreciation from doctors and specialists across Europe plus a trophy in Austria and the Gold Medal for the role played by the International Grand Prix Medical Service.

Today motor-racing has benefited from improvements in circuit safety. Death from crashes are rare. Drivers walk away unscathed from spectacular accidents. Medical aid on the track is a formality. The man appointed to handle this aspect is an elderly medic, 'Professor' Syd Watkins. He is highly competent, but I do wish he would drop the professional handle. It is pompous, out-of-place and impresses nobody. Far better to enjoy an Indian summer without Emeritus status. I am only glad he is spared the horrors of past years.

For the benefit of those who wondered what happened inside the Mobile Hospital during races, these are two of the routine reports.

SAMPLE MEDICAL REPORTS

The International Grand Prix Medical Service Unit arrived at Silverstone on the 11th July 1983, to cover practice session on the 12th and 13th July, and the British Grand Prix on July 14th.

A few minor cases were dealt with by the Silverstone Medical Headquarters on the two practice days, mainly medical checks of drivers involved in small shunts. They were discharged after examination by Dr Buckingham. On Saturday, 14th July, three drivers sustained serious injuries during the Saloon Car Race.

David Matthews and Dave Brodie were brought to the Hospital Unit, and Gavin Booth was dealt with in the Medical Headquarters adjoining the Mobile Hospital. All three drivers were in a serious condition. David Matthews was badly shocked, had fractured right ribs, chest injuries and possible leg injuries. He was treated by a team of four specialists. Dave Brodie had more serious injuries – a fractured left thigh, fracture to the left elbow, deep cut on chin, injury to the right shoulder caused by seat belt and was very shocked. As in the case of David Matthews, he was treated by another team of specialists. An anaesthetist gave Brodie anaesthetic whilst doctors dealt with the broken femur and splintered it; other fractures were immobilised and drips were administered to arrest shock.

The injuries sustained by Gavin Booth were fractured right femur, fractured left ankle, fractured left patella, head injuries, fracture of the jaw and was severely shocked. After treatment for his injuries, Booth was taken by ambulance to the Radcliffe Hospital, Oxford. From the major crash which occurred at the start of the Grand Prix, the Mobile Hospital Unit received on casualty – Andrea de Adamich, who sustained a fracture of the right ankle, possible fracture of the left ankle, and a deep cut on the bridge of nose and shock. Treatment was given by a team of doctors and he was taken by ambulance to the Northamption Hospital.

A driver from the F3 race was brought to the Unit as a result of a crash but after examination he was discharged.

The Hospital Unit treated a F3 mechanic following an electric shock which threw him into the air. He landed, face down, on a concrete road and sustained severe facial injuries and shock.

The Hospital also treated a serious burn to both feet of a Lotus mechanic, the injury being caused by boiling water.

On Friday afternoon a member of the public had a serious heart attack on the pits balcony, the St. John's ambulance driver and the Chief St John's officer plus two doctors were immediately in attendance.

The presence of the Mobile Hospital assured that first class medical and surgical facilities were available to doctors and surgeons under complete clinical conditions. Injured drivers were given correct medical and surgical attention according to their injuries and were able to travel safely to hospital. This could only result in a speedier recovery for all concerned, plus the fact that at least directly and indirectly life must have been saved by the presence of the hospital.

The Mobile Hospital arrived at Francorchamps on the 19th July 1973, for the 24 hour race. The doctors decided to position the Mobile Hospital at Stavelot as it was considered the most likely area for accidents.

On Friday, 20th July, the Hospital Unit received an Italian driver who had sustained injuries to his left shoulder and minor cuts. After examination and treatment he was taken to the hospital at Spa.

On Saturday, 21st July at 15.00 hours, the 24 Hour Race commenced. Intermitten rain showers throughout the race duration.

About midnight a message from control stated there had been a serious accident involving two cars. Staff on duty included the Chief Medical Officer, six other doctors and two anaesthetist. Thirty minutes later, two ambulances arrived with the news that both drivers had died in their cars.

The bodies were taken to a medical tent next to the Mobile Hospital.

The names of the drivers were JOISTEN (German) and DUBOIS (French).

Joisten had broken his neck, the chest wall had been depressed and the sternum was broken, both legs were broken in many places and the flesh had been ripped clean off the lower bones. Death was manly due to a broken neck on impact.

Dubois had also broken his neck. No other injuries were visible. The post mortem would probably reveal injuries that were not possible to detect on examination.

Both broken necks were identical, the neck was broken at the back where the crash helmet fitted.

At 13.00 hours, control reported another accident involving two cars The first driver to arrive was RAUS (Belgian). Examination showed he had broken his back. He was treated for shock, cuts and dressed. After being placed on a board and strapped down, he was transported by ambulance to Liège hospital.

The Italian driver, Larini, arrived as Raus was departing in the ambulance. He had serious head injuries and was in a coma. The whole of the right rib-cage was broken. Swelling of the chest indicated a severe Haemothorax, which had to be drained at once.

The patient was interbated and given oxygen. He was then infused with plasma, normal saline bicarbonate fluids and blood. An incision was made in the right chest wall and an underwater drainage was applied. A large quantity of blood was drained off, and the patient became more restful. He was then given HYDROCORTISONE and Valium injections to combat shock.

Having completed treatment the patient was taken to Liège Hospital by ambulance. The helicopter could not fly during the hours of darkness.

Had the International Grand Prix Hospital not attended this meeting, the Italian driver Larini would not have survived the journey by road to Liège Hospital. The driver with the broken spine would similarly have been damaged.

These two meetings emphasised once again that doctors and surgeon, however skilled, are unable to treat serious injuries unless the necessary equipment and clinical facilities are available. In the majority of cases the time lag between the crash and the hospital operating theatre is $1\frac{1}{2} - 2$ hours. In many cases this interval can result in death. On seven instances, the surgical facilities and medical equipment in the Mobile Hospital of the International Grand Prix Medical Service have bridged that gap and lives have been saved. Larini can be added to the list whilst Raus was safe guarded against grave implications.

Louis T. Stanley

Director General
INTERNATIONAL GRAND PRIX MEDICAL SERVICE 6th July, 1973
LTS/SRJ

11

Tragedies and the Aftermath

A sequel to the needless death of Jo Siffert was the setting-up of the Siffert Advisory Council. This became necessary because of the reluctance by the CSI to recognize the inefficiency of fire-fighting disciplines on the circuits. They remained satisfied with the policy of giving circuit owners the authority to organize their own fire-fighting units and procedures, in spite of damning evidence proving that drivers had died through mistakes and negligence of fire crews on duty.

The Council included men of vast experience as their credentials confirmed. It was the first authoritative body to tackle the fire hazard.

Below: The Council in session.

MEMBERS OF THE COUNCIL

Chairman:-
LOUIS T. STANLEY
Chairman of B.R.M. Limited
Director General of the International Grand Prix
Medical Service

F.C.A. SHIRLING, H Sc; C.Eng, M.I.Mech. E: M.I.
Fire Eng.
Engineering Inspector, H.M. Inspector of Fire
Service, Home Office

V. KIDD
Head of Fire Services (RAF), Ministry of Defence

E.T. HAYWARD, OBE; M.I. FIRE E.
H.M. Inspector of Fire Services, Home Office

J.E. LODGE, DFC
Chief Fire Services Officer, Civil Aviation
Authority

C. CAREY, BEM; M.I. Fire E.

Chief Fire Officer, Cambridge

H.B. FOX
Managing Director, Graviner Limited

G.E. FOLL, B.Sc; Ph.D.
Research Dept, Imperial Chemical Industries
Limited

D.E. CARTER
Sales Manager, 3M's Company Limited

D. RAWOON
Sales Manager, Bells Asbestos Limited

F.P. BREWER
Managing Director of HELI-JET Executive Limited

J.S. SANDERCOMBE – Secretary

In attendance: Messrs. Graham Hill and
Peter Gethin

Their brief was to assess how to tackle fire-hazards peculiar to motor-racing. At the outset every member was adamant that extinguishing a 50-gallon fuel fire in a car would only be an operation measured in seconds. This confidence was subjected to a series of rigorous tests and experiments at the Civil Aviation Fire School at Stansted and Graviners at Colnbrook. Special extinguishers were designed. Eventual findings showed that a running fuel fire involving 50 gallons of fuel had to be extinguished in 30 seconds. For a driver to survive, the first stage of the fire suppression operation had to be initiated within 15 seconds and the cockpit area isolated from the fire within a further 15 seconds. Circuit fire-fighting systems had to meet these parameters. An initial step was to site marshals at 65-yard intervals around the tracks.

Council recommendations were put to the test at Silverstone before television cameras. Among those present were FIA and CSI officials, Prince Metternich, GPDA representatives, circuit owners and members of the main Racing Clubs. Delegates came from Minnesota and flew back to the United States after the tests.

The fire was extinguished in 27 seconds. Only half the extinguishants were used.

Shortly afterwards Denny Hulme, then President of the Grand Prix Drivers Association, invited me to be Director of Circuit Safety with powers to ensure that the Siffert Advisory Council recommendations were carried out at future World Championship races. The Austrians were the first to conform.

There is no doubt that fire-fighting standards have improved, but when emergencies arise there is still no guarantee that the men using the equipment are up to the job. Donning a helmet does not mean his training has become professional. Today with pit stops lasting seconds, the drill has to be exact. High-pressure fuel lines have safeguards. Even so there have been mistakes. Purely by

Left: A marshal at Silverstone carrying the new portable spray equipment designed by the 3M Company to dispense Light Water foam at racing circuits. The equipment features two cylinders which have a capacity of four gallons of six percent Light Water AFFF concentrate. The concentrate is mixed with water and applied as a foam. The unique action of Light Water foam stems from its ability to make water float on flammable fuels which are lighter than water. The foam blanket spreads over the surface of the fuel. Aqueous solution drains from the foam bubbles and spreads over the surface to provide a vapour seal. This film-forming action plays a part in extinguishment and prevents reflash of the fuel.

chance a conflagration has been avoided. On the law of averages a fire-disaster will happen. Consequences could be dire. Perhaps then, the FIA will have second thoughts as to the wisdom of pandering to the demands of global television to infuse more excitement to a race even though it could cause loss of life. One factor must give a grain of comfort to those whose sons or husbands died in a racing car engulfed by flames. Burns specialists state that death, mercifully short, is caused not from burning but by suffocation through inhaling the searing hot gases which destroy the lungs.

Among the changes that have revolutionized, at times emasculated, motorracing, is one that used to be a potential nightmare. Team managers in the pits would be alerted by timekeepers that their car had not come round. Usually it would be mechanical problems. The exception was when a billowing cloud of

Below: British Airways firemen wearing specially designed backpacks attack the demonstration car fire.

black smoke could be seen in the distance, then the wait for news. Fire is a terrifying hazard. Occasionally such a crash happens in sight of the pits, like the 1978 Italian Grand Prix at Monza. Seconds after a hesitant starting procedure, 24 cars hurtled towards the artificial chicane that had been introduced to reduce speeds: there was a multiple pile-up. James Hunt's car was hit, Ronnie Peterson's Lotus was involved, spun off, clouted the guard-rail, exploded and burst into flames. Hunt leapt from his McLaren, kicked Peterson's seat-belt free, and with the help of a marshal, managed to drag the driver clear in spite of his legs being trapped. Reaction had been quick. In less than a minute, Peterson was taken away on a stretcher. Hunt's heroism was in vain. After a six-hour operation on his legs, Peterson died through blood clots restricting the flow of blood to the brain. So passed a brilliant driver, fearless on the track, but so gentle off, who could have been a genuine World Champion. At one time he wanted to join BRM. We had talks in the Loch Muhle hotel in Germany, but failed to reach agreement on contract details. Ronnie was yet another victim of the flames. Memories are short in this sport.

Right: Lorenzo Bandini, one of Italy's most promising young drivers.

Retrospective analysis of such crashes reveals how insensitive officials seemed to regard tragedy as inevitable incidents that should not interrupt a race. I think of that horrific accident at Le Mans when a wrecked car and engine scythed through lines of spectators leaving a sickening death-roll; of the Italian Grand Prix at Monza when von Trips died as well as eighteen spectators lining the protective fence; of Bandini's accident at Monte Carlo; of the crashes at Zandvoort when Piers Courage and Roger Williamson were burnt to death; of Jo Schlesser at Rouen. These are but some instances, when in spite of death, the races were allowed to continue. Callous official reactions suggested that motor-racing is potentially lethal and death just an aspect of a gladiatorial sport. Another disturbing feature was that so many accidents and fatalities were aggravated by, and on occasions due to, negligence on the part of circuit owners and officials. There were blatant refusals to carry out safety demands from the CSI and GPDA after assurances that the work had been done. This dismal record included every aspect of circuit safety for driver and spectator, plus fire-fighting equipment and professional training. In certain cases there should have been legal redress, but in

Below: The insensitive official attitude towards accidents and death allowed races to continue. Here Graham passes the burning Ferrari with Bandini trapped inside.

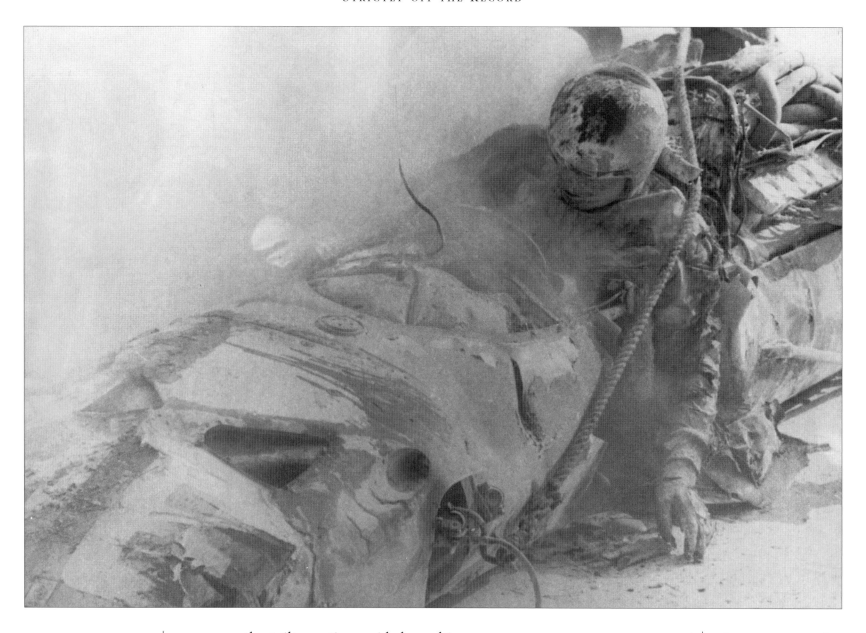

every one the guilty parties avoided penalties, or censure.

Take the Bandini crash at Monte Carlo in 1967. His Ferrari hit the barriers at the chicane, overturned, caught fire, Bandini receiving extensive burns from which he died. The marshals on duty lacked emergency equipment. Courageous spectators had to help. The Italian driver was spreadeagled on the ground without immediate medical aid. As the race was allowed to continue, an improvised water-ambulance had to be used. The delay was costly.

The Roger Williamson crash at Zandvoort was unbelievably inefficient. On the eighth lap, the left front tyre on Williamson's March exploded. The car hit the outer guard-rail, which buckled through having been set in fine sand. It ricocheted back on the track, finishing upside down on the apex of the right-hander. The left-hand fuel tank was ruptured causing a small fire. Purley stopped his car and rushed to help. A few yards away was a fire-tender, but as the race was still on, the fire crew refused to move. Marshals with fire-extinguishers refused to help Purley in his attempts to right the upturned car. For two laps, very nearly three

Above: Tragic example of what happens when rescue services fail to take immediate action.

Left: Piers Courage was another brilliant driver who lost his life in a burning car.

minutes, he struggled. The fire then increased in intensity. Purley seized a fire-extinguisher from an immobile marshal. Spectators tried to help but were driven back by police with dogs, who did the same with Purley. All this time Williamson had been calling out, only to die in the flames. It was the worst kind of inhumane cruelty seen in motor-racing. Yet there was no redress from officialdom.

Three years earlier the same inefficiency was demonstrated when Piers Courage on the same section of the track crashed and was engulfed in flames. Fire-fighting methods were sub-standard. Overall directive laid down that in the event of an accident, the circuit car would go to the crash-point with an official and a doctor to assess the incident. If there was a fire, the fire-truck would be summoned. Such delay ignored the fact that all this time the driver was trapped in the flames. On this occasion I went to the scene of the crash with the Chief of Police after the race had ended. The only sign of the wrecked car was a mound of sand and thin plumes of smoke. As to Piers, I leave it to your imagination. Comforting Sally was very traumatic.

The Jo Schlesser tragedy at Rouen was another example of official insensitivity, and short-sighted planning. Before the French Grand Prix practice session had ended, there was an incident when a car had a small fire. There were no firemen on duty. The fire-extinguishers did not work. The official excuse was that full procedures would only operate on race-day, as the men were not available on practice sessions! Jo Schlesser, the local veteran, was anxious to make his Formula One début. Earlier I had received a letter asking if he could drive a BRM in the World Championship race. I had doubts whether he could handle the machinery. Enthusiasm was not enough. For his sake I refused the request. Honda foolishly gave him a car that was unreliable. There had been pre-race doubts about safety standards in Rouen. At a GPDA meeting at Nürburgring, certain recommendations were made. The officials were asked to consider the straight wooded sections where there would be slip-streaming with no protection for drivers or spectators. Erecting Armco barriers on both sides of the track at the entrance and exit at all corners on the uphill section would be a safeguard, also from the pits to the hairpin. The hairpin at the end of the main straight was dangerously rough, being surfaced with concrete. Another question-mark was the corner where permanent concrete bollards were a lethal hazard even though protected by straw

bales. Jim Clark later suggested specific modifications in a personal letter. One sector, he emphasised, was particularly dangerous. That was where Schlesser was killed.

The suggestions were examined and approved by the CSI Safety Committee at meetings in Paris and Frankfurt and sent to Rouen organizers, who gave the assurance that the modifications would be carried out. Nothing was done. As to what happened when Schlesser crashed, I quote an eyewitness account by Edward McDonough of Chingford:

'I was standing at the fence, approximately 50 feet from the corner, and had an unobstructed view. The Honda came down the hill not appearing to be entering the bend faster than anyone else, and the engine cut out. Schlesser was sufficiently behind the others for the silence to be noticeable. This has been confirmed by several friends who were farther up the hill, looking down towards where the crash took place. He lost control and went into the bank, the petrol exploded, the car dropped on to the track, and, although I fell to the ground, I was aware that a few seconds went by before the car was engulfed in flames.

'I was on my feet 60 to 90 seconds after the petrol exploded, and could see fire marshals standing at the corner in asbestos suits without gloves or protective helmets, making no effort to get near the car. Throughout the earlier races they did not wear full equipment, nor did they pay much attention to the track.

'The small fire extinguishers on hand did not work, as only a trickle of chemical came out. Several minutes went by before the hoses from the fire engines were used, and, of course, water had little effect on the burning material of the car. It actually caused it to flare up more. Approximately 20 minutes after the track was cleared, a red van appeared coming down the track, Jackie Ickx having to swerve as the van began to cross the track in front of him. The van then parked for 10 minutes on the apex of the bend, so visibility was blocked before crossing.

'It is very easy to criticize afterwards, but several facts demand action. The fire marshals appeared to have no idea as to how they should deal with this type of tragedy. The equipment on hand was ineffective, and some of it did not function. Foam instead of water should have been available.

'Marshals in the post were very young looking, several had girl friends, and one girl dropped a beverage can on to the track and this had to be retrieved. Prior to the start, spectators placed themselves outside the fencing on the corner and refused to move when a marshal asked them to do so. It seems obvious that if Schlesser had gone off a fraction of a second earlier, he would have easily gone into the crowd, and certainly the marshals and equipment could not have coped with this. I don't know if poor Schlesser could have been saved, but there was a brief period when this might have been possible. It seems wrong to allow marshals like these to man such posts.'

Another distressing feature was the insensitive attitude by the French officials to his wife, Annie Schlesser. When her husband died in the flames, she was unable to get confirmation of his death or where he had been taken. It was two hours before she was told. By that time she was on the verge of total collapse; her 12-year old daughter became very distressed. The Frenchman's blackened corpse was in the mobile hospital. The next few hours were traumatic, comforted by my wife Jean and Betty Brabham during the night. The following morning they were informed that Annie would be taken to Paris by ambulance. If she became hysterical, a strait-jacket would be used. We offered to take mother and daughter to

Left: Straw bales looked impressive, but in themselves posed a safety hazard.

Right: Jo Siffert, seen here with Jean Stanley, responded to the power and reliability of the BRM. A potential World Champion, he was elated at taking pole position from Jackie Stewart at Brands Hatch, only to lose his life through appalling rescue attempts after he crashed.

Paris in our car. Even then red tape insisted that a medical document had to be obtained from the doctor who had attended Jo. Guy Ligier provided the answer. He took the document to Rouen, then flew the Schlessers to their home. Officials should learn that their responsibilities do not end when a driver is buried. Only then does the humane side begin. The number of racing widows who have suffered hardship and breakdowns after their husbands were killed is considerable. The sport has a responsibility to its own people.

I come now to the tragic crash at Brands Hatch when Jo Siffert was burnt to death. It is one that concerns us deeply for it was the only time that a driver had died at the wheel of a BRM. Jo at the peak of his form and in a powerful competitive car was in pole position, ahead of Jackie Stewart. Many facts came to light at the inquest at Tonbridge Police Station.

The coroner, Douglas Thomson, described the fire-fighting at the circuit as hopeless and well-nigh criminal. The pronouncement was not exaggerated. Seldom has there been such a series of disastrous mistakes.

Left: Phil Hill surveys his burnt car after clouting a straw bale at Zeltweg in Austria.

Behave or Else

Crowd control at motor-races is a permanent worry to officials. No country has the answer. Silverstone, for instance, prides itself on keeping a clean sheet, yet when spectators were hyped-up by nationalistic jingo by the media about the chances of Nigel Mansell winning the British Grand Prix, crowds milled on to the track before the race had ended, all anxious to be at the champagne squirting ritual. Censure followed but had little effect.

Above: Officials at Monza, where prompt and heroic response failed to save Ronnie Peterson in a multiple pile-up in 1978.

Right: Gendarmes on the Rouen circuit – where inefficiency and poor safety measures contributed to Jo Schlesser's death.

Left: Political unrest meant that police armed with tear-gas and guns were deployed at the 1970 Mexican Grand Prix.

Top: These jackbooted troopers seem fairly relaxed about their security role at Estoril, seaside setting for the Portuguese Grand Prix.

Above: Gendarmes again – this time at Le Mans, where 83 spectators died when a car somersalted over a safety barrier in 1955.

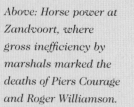

Above: Horse power at Zandvoort, where gross inefficiency by marshals marked the deaths of Piers Courage and Roger Williamson.

Above right: Security in Argentina involves helmeted troops armed with automatic rifles. If only all safety measures were as thorough!

Right: Francorchamps: Jackie Stewart's ordeal here in 1966 led to the foundation of the International Grand Prix Medical Service.

Above: A more durable car than those on the circuit is used by Belgian troops intent on keeping the peace at Francorchamps.

Top and right: The mass deployment of motor-cycle cops and troops shows laudable concern for spectators' safety. But, all too often, the behaviour of officials who seem to regard drivers as gladiators in a lethal battle has led to the loss of lives.

12

American Influences

The emergence of the United States of America as a pioneering force in motor racing was due in part to four men – Carl Fisher, Arthur Newby, Frank Wheeler and Jim Allison – who at the beginning of the century planned to construct a motor-racing track with facilities for testing automobiles. On February 9th, 1909 theory became reality. A company was formed named the Indianapolis Motor Speedway with a capital of 250,000 dollars. 320 acres of land were bought, sufficient for two tracks, one five miles, the other, half that size. The smaller scheme was preferred. The stadium was described as a bowl or oval, somewhat misleading as the area was a rectangle. The intended circuit design had four bends, slightly banked, linked by four straights. Track width would be 52 feet on the straights that widened to 62 feet on the four bends. Track surface to be gravel packed with earth. Progress was rapid, the work being completed by June 5th, 1909.

Surprisingly the first event was a balloon race. The novelty appealed. 3,500 people were in the stadium, whilst an estimated 40,000 enjoyed the freebie outside the gates. The inaugural motor race was held two months later. Facilities were ahead of their time, with grandstands, subways giving access to the centre of the circuit, and a landing-strip for aircraft. Remember this was 1909. There was a set-back. The tar and gravel surface of the track was ripped up by the cars and the day marred by death. William Bourque, mechanics Kelhun and Holcoln, and two spectators lost their lives, the forerunners of the grim toll that would be taken by Indianapolis.

The track was resurfaced using clay bricks, hence the nickname *Brickyard*. It entailed laying some 3,250,000 bricks in 63 days, an average of over 50,000 bricks a day. The track reopened in December; highlights were speed records set up by Louis Strang in a 200-hp Fiat. Five months later the Motor Speedway held a three day meeting featuring 42 races, 60,000 spectators enjoying the jamboree. Planning ahead, the four pioneers decided to concentrate in future on only one race of 500 miles with substantial prize-money. There was a qualifying requirement. Every car had to be capable of producing speeds of 75 mph-plus. 40 cars lined up for the first '500'. The race was won by Ray Harroun in a Marmon Wasp. One death. Sam Dickson, a mechanic was thrown from Arthur Greiner's car against the reinforced concrete walls sited in front of the grandstands for spectator safety, even though lethal for divers . . .

In 1927 the Indianapolis Speedway was bought by Eddie Rickenbacker. Again sweeping changes. The brick surface disappeared under a layer of asphalt. Ownership changed in 1945 when Anton Hulman Jr revolutionized the financial set-up. He established the '500' as one of the greatest races in the calendar. There is a dark side. The race has claimed a terrible toll of lives. In the current trend for race safety without detracting from the thrills of a race, it is wrong that the macho Indianapolis attitude should persist. We have outgrown the Spanish bull-fight mentality.

Over the years Indianapolis has attracted motor racing's famous personalities. One man stands out. A controversial character if ever there was one, Andy Granatelli's charmed life survived the perils of hot-rod racing. Scarred for life by innumerable horrific crashes, he was given the exclusive 'badge 500', and became 'Mister 500', a gesture applauded by the racing world

Those who imagined that the return of Formula One racing to the United States would be warmly welcomed were surprised by the luke-warm reaction. The package is not a 'natural'. There are several possible reasons. Some Americans distrust publicity-hype claiming Formula One cars are technically superior to what is on offer in the States and dismiss the claim as rubbish. Obviously the racing will be good with global television coverage, but why import a bunch of comparatively unknown foreigners with varying skills when America already has a packed fixture-list catering for all levels of motor-racing, with Indianapolis as its flagship?

Purists have no doubt about its status and importance. Until a few years ago this was emphasized. After the Indy-500 was staged in a blaze of publicity, the Speedway was not used for the rest of the year. It was exclusive. Americans cherish their icons like the Augusta Masters, showpiece of American golf. Organization for both events leaves nothing to chance, Augusta being more meticulous and self-critical. After the winner's green jacket is donned and the crowds melt away, post-mortems are held. One year I was present after professionals complained that the greens had been like lightning. It was true. Stimpmeter readings showed a speed of 12 feet against an average on the tournament circuit of between 6 and 7. In other words, suicidal speed. Without hesitation the Committee agreed that

Below: Louis Wagner drove a massive 12-litre Fiat to victory in the first Grand Prix of the United States, run over a 25-mile course (prepared by convict chain-gangs) at Savannah, Georgia on 26th November 1908.

certain greens, though immaculate and weed-free, should be ploughed up before the next season. Such is the determination to achieve near perfection that the founder, Bobby Jones, visualized.

Indianapolis, with similar high standards, maintained their format over the years until 1994 when purists were upset at having to stage the NASCAR Winston Cup race. But it has become a tremendous crowd-puller and now ranks second to the Daytona-500. The Brickyard hosts two classics, the established Indy-500 and the rookie Brickyard-400 event.

It is fortunate that harmony reigns, for American motor-racing archives record many instances of inner rivalry. I pick out 1908, the year that marked bitter in-fighting between the conventional Automobile Club of America and, by comparison, the brasher Automobile Association of America. The ACA, as the older club and representative of America on the AIACR, predecessor of the FIA, held the Vanderbilt Cup race on Long Island with the approval of ACA. The bickering ended when the ACA announced that the first Grand Prix of the United States would be held on Thanksgiving Day, 26th November, 1908 at Savannah in Georgia.

European racing marques responded. France had de Dietrich, Clement-Bayard, and Renault. Italy entered Fiat and Itala. Germany had Benz. America added modified stock cars. Technical details produced a formula restricting the piston area to a total of 755 square cm, minimum weight 2,425 lbs. Most of the cars were 4-cylinders, the piston area restriction had a maximum bore of 1.5 inches. The Fiats were typical of the 1908 Grand Prix machines, ie; 4 cylinders, bore and stroke of 155 ¥ 160, displacement of 12 litres, gearbox 53.3 inches, wheelbase 108.3 and approximate weight, 2650 lbs.

The race was planned with American thoroughness. Special trains increased crowd attendance to over 100,000. Crowd control was the responsibil-

Below: 50th Anniversary and reenactment of early Watkins Glen races, Sept. 1998. Bill Milliken, with Doug, in the car he raced in WGGP in 1949.

ity of 1000 troops. 30 doctors were on duty. 160 marshals were detailed for flag duties. Telephone service was installed, giving immediate telegraph coverage. And remember this was 1908, the year when Ford's first new Model T was produced in Detroit, replacing the existing Model A, and fulfilled Henry Ford's promise to produce a motor car "for the great multitude".

The Savannah course was 25.13 miles long with some 35 corners. According to the drivers, dangerous and fast. Injuries were anticipated. Mechanics organized a fund from voluntary donations of a hundred dollars apiece for the next of kin should a mechanic be killed. The first payment was made when a mechanic was killed in practice. Twenty cars were on the grid, starting at one-minute intervals. After a gruelling race Louis Wagner was the winner at an average speed of 65.08 mph and race distance of 402.08 miles.

An incident after the race showed how instructions that the course should be kept clear were carried out. René Hanriot in a Benz drove back to the pits in the reverse direction of the course. Soldiers on duty did not know the race had ended, ordered Hanriot to stop. He ignored the command, and at the next corner, a Captain Davant fired bullets into the tyres, gas tank, and just missed the driver.

The finishing order of America's first Grand Prix records the pioneers and their cars:

1.	Louis Wagner	Fiat	6.20.31
2.	Victor Hémery	Benz	6.11.27
3.	Felice Nazzaro	Fiat	6.18.47
4.	René Hanriot	Benz	6.26.12
5.	Lucien Hautvast	Clement-Bayard	6.34.06
6.	Louis Strang	Renault	6.43.37
7.	Victor Rigal	Clement-Bayard	6.45.43
8.	Henri Fournier	Itala	6.46.32
9.	Ralph de Palma	Fiat	6.51.34
10.	Arthur Duray	de Dietrich	14 laps
11.	Seymour	Simplex	14 laps

Fastest Lap: 21 mins 36 seconds 69.80 mph. de Palma, Fiat.

Watkins Glen has also contributed richly to American racing history. In 1948 they held the first Sports Car Grand Prix of the United States, at that time an innovation, for road racing was a novelty and sports cars as such unknown.

Drivers were used to competing on the Indianapolis closed-oval or county fair dirt tracks. Cameron Argetsinger was the man who made it possible. The Glen could provide a genuine road race over surfaces of varying conditions. The course was planned to start in the main street of Watkins Glen, up Corning Hill, then through the State Park, across farmlands with the finishing line in Franklin Street: eight laps over a 6.6-mile course. The prospect appealed to the public. 10,000 spectators attended. The initial entry of 36 cars was cut to 15 after qualifying. The grid consisted of MGs, an Alfa-Romeo and Briggs Cunningham's BU Mercedes. Drivers were drawn from wealthy amateurs, including Sam and Miles Collier, George Weaver of New England and the two Glen legends, Bill Milliken and Cameron. The race itself became a knife-edge affair between Franz Griswold in the Alfa-Romeo and the Mercedes of Briggs Cunningham. Victory went to Griswold, who also won the Junior Prix on the same day. Ten cars finished, including

Argetsinger, Alec Ulman, famous at Sebring, Smith Hempstone Oliver, curator of the Smithsonian Institute, and the burly racing historian, Charles Lytle.

Continuing this race brought rewards and headaches. Spectators doubled in number, likewise the number of entries. There were tragedies with both driver and spectator deaths. Lloyd's of London declined to insure the race unless crowd control was assured. An alternative lay-out was substituted; a rectangle of roads in the town of Dix served as a stopgap circuit from 1953 to 1955. Bill Milliken solved the difficulties. With a team from the Cornell Engineering Department and approval of the Grand Prix Corporation, 550 acres of land was purchased, the acreage being developed into a 2.3-mile circuit on the hill above the Glen. Building schedule cut it fine. Paving surface was completed the night before the first practice, but crumbling road surfaces caused windscreen shattering and a cable from SCCA president advised drivers not to compete. To the relief of those who had invested 200,000 dollars private capital in non-stock certificates of indebtedness, the drivers voted to ignore the advice.

Right: Louis Stanley with Cameron Argetsinger – one of the most respected figures in American motor-racing.

SCCA safety demands were eventually resolved. Under Argetsinger's guidance, the Glen introduced a series of improvements that included the Technical Building and Kendall Service Centre housing cars and mechanics, and the Paddock Club. Concrete grandstands were sited by the S-bends, bleachers at principal viewing sites. Safety standards meant installing 52,000 linear feet of guardrail, culminating in 1971 with a 3.4-million dollar sale that confirmed the Glen's international status. With new pits, tower for press and time-keepers, new start-finish area, circuit widened and repaved, plus another mile of curves and straights, concession stands, water wells, restroom facilities, spectator tunnel crossing one section of the circuit, plus improved drainage systems. It had taken twenty-five years, but Watkins Glen had achieved its target of racing maturity.

Credit was due to the sheer enthusiasm of its supporters. Having known all the circuits of the world, my favourite without hesitation is Watkins Glen. Maybe coloured by BRM victories in the U.S. title honours, its appeal was the real community enthusiasm for the sport, maybe old-fashioned and dated, but nevertheless organized and efficient. As director of circuit safety, I made official inspections. The Grand Prix Drivers' Association markings were always high. Race organization was directed by a eleven-member committee who served without pay. 300 volunteer workers had box lunches of sandwiches cut in the Methodist Church, the service rotating among the local churches. Official accreditation done in the village classroom with the wives and girl friends of officials handing

out passes. Schoolteachers were at the ticket-gates, civic organizations were responsible for concession booths, seniors sold programmes. Scrutineering, marshals and fire-fighting units relied on community volunteers. Louis Peck was the liaison-link. Schuyler Hospital Association organized the Watkins Glen Festival with Dick Smothers as grand marshal of the parade. Every winner of the race was embraced by the chosen Queen of the Festival who became Miss United States Grand Prix. On display was the traditional trophy for this race, a silver bowl designed by the early American silversmith, Paul Revere.

Success at the Glen was shared by the people behind the scenes. The "Voice of the Glen" was John Duvall, calm and informative. No sign of the spluttering, raucous commentating of today's races. One lady in particular who presided was Jean Argetsinger, wife of the Glen stalwart. The last time I was at their home in Burdett, the news came through she had been re-elected trustee of the Southern Tier Library System at a meeting at Lodge-in-the-Green in Painted Post. Everything was on a rural note by genuine enthusiasts. Some 28 years have passed. I was saddened to hear from Cameron that his wife had suffered a stroke towards the end of 1998, but several months later she made a full recovery, and was again presiding over the board of the Watkins Glen Public Library's Motor Racing Research Library. In that sense the Glen is a time-capsule. Life goes on in orderly fashion untouched by sleaze and scandal. Would we could say the same for this side of the Atlantic.

Unfortunately sentiment does not figure in the Millennium. Officialdom, quirks, financial baits and greed mean that change is inevitable. Finding an alternative site for the United States has been unfortunate. The Detroit jungle of concrete office skyscrapers was an unimaginative choice, likewise a glorified Las Vegas car-park. With the resumption of the race Bernie Ecclestone now decides where it is to be held. Watkins Glen was a possibility, but Cameron told me the financial demands were ludicrous. He declined. So Ecclestone began meaningful talks with Tony George. Final agreement was reached. The U.S. Grand Prix would be held at the Indianapolis Motor Speedway. A detailed letter from Cameron summed it up. Relevant quotes are pert. "Bernie succeeded because of sheer brass balls" – the phrase can be interpreted as you like! He goes on: "I believe Tony George understands what is involved. I am glad there finally will be a U.S. Grand Prix and at a venue with the tradition, knowledge and wherewithal to do it justice. If the Grand Prix cannot be here at Watkins Glen, it should be at Indianapolis." In 1998 the Glen celebrated its 50th Anniversary in style.

When it comes to compiling a list of pioneers of American motor-racing, it has to be a personal choice. Standing on a winner's rostrum is not the most important factor. Choice embraces the personalities around whom the sport evolved and reflects the decades in which they lived. They add colour to the pages of history.

PHIL HILL

Phil Hill is that rare creature – a quiet American. Unobtrusively walking about the pit area, few people realize that here is the first American to win the 24 Hours race at Le Mans, the first American to win three times at Sebring, the first American to win a modern championship Grand Prix and the first American to win the World Championship. In spite of this remarkable record, Phil Hill is relatively unrecognized by racing crowds. He does nothing to alter this anonymity. In many ways it is his wish, but even in self-imposed eclipse, he is among the élite to be judged on their level. His international reputation can never be lost.

I wonder sometimes whether the tragedy that marred the climax of the 1961 World Championship affected his attitude to racing. When the Italian Grand Prix ended, Phil Hill was World Champion but congratulations were muted by the thought that his team-mate, Wolfgang von Trips, had been killed. He never hit the headlines again in Formula One. His relationship with Enzo Ferrari deteriorated. About this time Phil made a decision that influenced his career. He asked to come over from Los Angeles for talks. I met him in The Dorchester in London, and matched the Italian terms to join BRM. The discussion continued in my home in Cambridge. He said that Ferrari had given several assurances. He would be No.1 in the team with the best engine and so on. Knowing the Commendatore's devious ways of manipulating his drivers, I suggested Phil should be cautious. He decided to stay at Maranello. BRM won the World Championship. Phil was ditched by the team. Had he joined BRM, further Formula One success might have come his way.

Not many people know the home life of Phil Hill or appreciate his varied talents. In Santa Monica he came to life. Strikingly designed and furnished with rare taste, he spent a great deal of time in his music room. The walls were lined with shelves crammed with cylinders. In his collection are every type of pianola, musical boxes and automata; the sum total reflects the tastes of a connoisseur. His knowledge of classical music is extensive. Name a tune and he can produce it under conditions of acoustic perfection. In those days Phil was a confirmed bachelor but he did not let his self-imposed status deprive him of creature comforts. The kitchen was planned and designed so that every known mechanical device and gadget was incorporated. What was more, he knew how they all worked. A very attractive American girl changed his mind. He married and lived happy ever after. She in turn acquired a well-trained husband!

Right: Phil Hill with Louis Stanley in Beverly Hills, Hollywood, after winning the World Championship at Monza.

RICHIE GINTHER

Richie Ginther's outlook on life was light-hearted and frivolous, but the mood changed when work had to be done. During his stay with BRM the little Californian played an important role in technical development of the car. In one way the American was disadvantaged through being in the same team as Graham Hill. Both were friendly, team spirit was good, but it coincided with Hill touching peak form. However hard Ginther tried, Hill had the edge on him. It was not that Hill's car was better prepared or more competitive, it was his degree of skill. Ginther's courage and tenacity were highly developed. Three times he had bad crashes. Each time recovery was hastened by sheer determination to resume racing. Convalescence after a crash at Aintree was maybe helped by pretty nurses, but the way he persevered to regain muscle-strength after being badly burnt when the BRM went up in flames whilst testing amazed the medics at Stamford. Instead of a routine recovery, he drove one of his finest races in the Monaco Grand Prix. He had several seconds during his stay with BRM and in 1962 was runner-up in the World Championship. His third crash was at Monza in a Honda which saw him in an Italian hospital run by nuns. He looked in a bad way. To get more enlightened treatment, I arranged to fly him to London. Three days later in St Thomas's Hospital he again surprised the doctors by saying he was returning to California at the end of the week and intended to drive a Honda in the next Grand Prix. It was worth it. He recorded his first and only Grand Prix victory. His association with Dan Gurney might have been productive but feeling he had reached the end of the line, he retired. His all-embracing grin was sadly missed. Instead he enjoyed archaeological trips to Death Valley.

Left: This gesture did not have special significance!

AMERICAN HALL OF FAME

A. J. Foyt... one of the most colourful figures on the circuits.
Parnelli Jones... legend in American stock car and Indianapolis-style racing.
Andy Granatelli... 'Mister 500'... that says it all.
Masten Gregory... remembered for his rich Kansas City drawl and thick horn spectacles.
Made his mark on the European scene in the small rear-engined Coopers.

Other names that should be included must be **Ralph de Palma: Ray Harroun: Wilbur Shaw: Alec Ulmann: Lee Petty: Mark Donohue: Louis Meyer: Tommy Milton: Rodger Ward: Lee Roy Yarbrough: Richard Petty: Frank Lockhart: Barney Oldfield: Ted Horn: Peter Revson;** plus many others, often unknown in Europe, but each one an ambassador for the American sport.

Right: Bill Milliken, veteran American driver and engineer extraordinaire.

Far right: Outstanding U.S. motivators - Alec Ulmann (left) of Sebring fame and Harry Holman, linked with Indianapolis.

Right: Carroll Shelby, who introduced American drivers to the European scene.

Left: Mario Andretti, arguably the greatest American racing driver with a spectacular career, collecting every major honour in both Europe and the United States. Has survived innumerable crashes and seems to be indestructible. He is a figurehead and a touchstone of American motor-racing.

Above: Dan Gurney, another American landmark. Successful on both sides of the Atlantic with an impressive list of major victories. Retiring from cockpit motorsport, his cars have been highly competitive on the U.S. scene. His stay with BRM was invigorating. He has an air of perpetual youthfulness and an expansive grin like an American Cheshire cat

Right: The Unser family are outstanding in American motor-racing history. It is arguable which of the two brothers- Al or Bobby- is better. Both seem indestructible. Bobby (right) drove for BRM. On a visit to Cambridge we walked down King's Parade as students came out of lectures. Every pretty girl was whistled-up by Bobby. I later referred to him in print as 'a natural ornithologist!'

13

Anniversaries of Motor Racing

There were two outstanding events in the autumn of 1998. The first was the celebration of the 50th anniversary of the Goodwood circuit; the second a similar reminder of 50 years of Silverstone, home of British motor-racing. They made a memorable finale to an eventful season. Compared with its past record, the transformation at Silverstone has been remarkable. Even more so are plans for future development, that include monorail trains circulating from car parks to the circuit; Silverstone bypass, already given Government approval, that will eliminate holdups stretching for miles; big-screen television; an imaginative BRDC clubhouse at Woodcote. Spectators will benefit from technology.

Goodwood in contrast was a festival of nostalgic memories. The Earl of March and his staff had turned back the clock. The Goodwood circuit had not been used for 32 years, but against the backdrop of reconstructed pits, grandstands and paddock, a time-warp illusion had been created, an effect that the Earl's grandfather, the 7th Duke of Richmond and Gordon would have approved.

Traditionalist in every way, Freddie was immensely proud of Goodwood's historical background. He told me that it was appropriate that the London Season, that began in May with the opening of the Royal Academy, should draw to a close against the leafy background of Charlton Wood and the Downs. King Edward VII described Goodwood as a garden-party with racing tacked on. Freddie acknowledged the description by saying that racing at Newmarket was big business, at Goodwood a leisured pastime with crowds in holiday mood on Trundle Hill.

History was made at Goodwood in many ways. Freddie March, as he then was, recalled several instances; of a unique hunt on 16th January, 1738, when a dawn meeting at Charlton Wood saw hounds locate an old bitch fox in East Dean Wood shortly before 8 o'clock. Ten hours and five minutes later, the kill was made a couple of miles north of Arundel, The prototype of the Goodwood Cup took place in the Spring of 1801 when the 3rd Duke gave permission for members of the Goodwood Hunt, officers of the Sussex militia, to run a number of two-mile heats. The following year the first public Goodwood race-meeting was held with 16 races in three days for prize money of £1,001. Of many characters, Lord Cavendish-Bentinck was singled out. He won a race in 1824 when riders wore cocked hats. He complained that in dry weather the last half-mile influenced running so he gave orders for the turf to be covered with several inches of mould topped by turf. Apparently it did the trick. Freddie remarked that people in those days were more patient. In the Stewards Cup, a field of 40 was 30 minutes late going to the start to which was added a further delay of 70 minutes.

Similar patience was needed when the post-war Goodwood Estate inherited an abandoned aerodrome that was still under Government control. Visualizing that the aerodrome perimeter track could be incorporated into a motor-racing substitute for Brooklands, Freddie March had first to cut through red-tape restrictions and get permission from the Ministries of Air War, Town and Country Planning, Agriculture, Works, Supply and Fuel, Board of Trade, plus Sussex & County and Chichester Councils. After that reconstruction plans could be examined.

Freddie's enthusiasm for engineering and motor-racing was practical. In April 1924 he took a job at Bentley Motors at a rate of ninepence an hour and was known to workmates as Mr. Settrington, one of the family names. Passionate about small cars, he began racing in 1929. It was short-lived. Nine races in all – but including victory in the 1930 BRDC 500-Miles with Sammy Davis as co-driver. This race was reported by a wag as the '2 Earls and 30 Misters Race'. He was also President of the Light Car Club founded by Hugh Nevill-Davies, also of the March motor business and became recognized as a car body stylist. In 1935 his father, paralysed by polio, died and Freddie became the 9th Duke of Richmond and Gordon.

Left: Reg Parnell, who tamed the V-16's power.

Returning to the Goodwood Anniversary Meeting, it was an occasion to savour. From our point of view, it was strange to recall that moment in 1948 when Reg Parnell drove the BRM V-16 to its first victory and Froilan Gonzalez's handling of this powerful machine in the Goodwood Trophy. There were also V-16s in the paddock, and various types of BRM circulating on the circuit, including Jackie Stewart wearing resurrected blue overalls for the occasion. Spectators applauded the appearance of Stirling Moss revisiting the scene of the crash that ended his Grand Prix ambitions; warmed to the spirited driving by Jack Brabham at the wheel of the Cooper-Climax in which he won the 1960 World Championship; veterans like Phil Hill, Dan Gurney and Roy Salvadori were greeted with enthusiasm; John Surtees in benign fashion introduced his perky youngster to us in the paddock; Derek Bell demonstrated the skill that brought five Le Mans 24-hour victories. Driving Steve O'Rourke's Maserati-engined Cooper, he won the Richmond Trophy in style and the Spirit of the Meeting Award. Afterwards he joined us for tea with the aside, 'Had I done this twenty-five years ago you might have offered me a BRM contract!' How right he was. Other veterans included Frank Gardner in a Cobra, Danny Sullivan, former Indycar champion, John Fitzpatrick cool and unruffled, even Damon Hill.

Another innovation intended to recapture the feel of the time was the request that gentlemen should wear jacket and tie in the paddock. Stewards donned bowler hats that in some cases were far from flattering. Ladies were asked to consider unearthing garments of the period. Theoretically acceptable, and many females did try, it overlooked the sad fact that figures do change with the passage of years. In one case the seams were over-strained. An embarrassing moment occurred when I complimented a lady on the 'old' look, only to be told that her garb was very much '98 vintage. Various group photographs were taken. One female who used to figure prominently on the racing scene said that if I was tempted to use the picture in a book, would I mind taking a former likeness instead, 'Time works havoc with facial lines!'

The remark reminded me of an occasion when I met Elizabeth Arden over drinks in the Savoy Hotel, London. I half expected a Maupassant gamine, the personification of what the medievalists portrayed in stained glass and wood-carving as luxury. Instead I was greeted by someone petite, barely 5 feet 4 inches, trim, attractive and not young. I was surprised to learn she opened her first salon as long ago as 1910. Her skin was gently wrinkled with laughter lines. The following day produced an interesting postscript. A package of male Arden toiletries arrived for me at the Dorchester Hotel, followed by a visit of an Arden executive from the Bond Street shop. Charmingly she enquired whether I had received prints of photographs taken during the dinner the night before. When told that nothing had arrived, she asked if I would let her have any prints taken of Elizabeth Arden. As a personal reminder of the evening she had brought a studio portrait of the lady in question. I asked why the interest in these particular prints and was told it

would be contrary to Company policy if photographs of their founder were in circulation showing signs of old age and the inevitable facial wrinkles. The photograph I was given had been taken years earlier and had no lines or blemishes. The face was as smooth as a billiard ball. I declined the offer. When the Savoy photographs arrived, Elizabeth Arden looked far more attractive than the touched-up likeness. Her private mask was far superior to the public relations version.

The same might be said of the apprehensive racing female. Her current likeness is just as attractive as the days when she wanted reflected publicity. Not taking risks, both versions are omitted, but she should remember that the image of mature beauty is not determined by a pot of cream.

The Earl of March and his staff must have been satisfied by the results of careful planning. The bonus was the glorious weather, one of the warmest days of a disappointing summer. They successfully recreated an era. As an aside, it was good to meet again Canon Lionel Webber, Chaplain to Her Majesty the Queen and the British Racing Drivers Club, who blessed the track prior to the start of racing against a background of Spitfires demonstrating war-time skills in the skies. Watson's genuine enthusiasm for motor-racing is refreshing. Such a change from so many clerics who spend their time emerging from toilets, vestries and confessional cubicles. It is just as well that the Almighty has a sense of humour!

Left: The thunderous start of the 1952 Goodwood Trophy, with Gonzales at the wheel of the BRM V-16 (5)

14

Looking Forward

The Millennium invites us to speculate what the future has in store. Applied to motor-racing, and Formula One in particular, the outlook is far from promising. Before indulging in crystal-gazing, the theme of the Millennium is threatening to be an over-sell. Cynics with a Socratic turn of mind point out it is impossible to determine the precise moment when a thing ceases to be 'new' and becomes 'old'. Even the heartiest of revellers will find it difficult to pin-point how 12.05 am on January 1st was essentially different from 11.55 pm of the day before. Nor is it. Astronomers inform us to the tick when year merges into year, century into century, but the time-division is a creature of our own devising. The Millennium as such has no definition outside our imagination.

In the world of Grand Prix racing, little will change, *Michael Schumacher* will continue to be conscious of his own ability and lack of it in others. Brilliant, but temperamentally flawed. Never intentionally rude, from time to time has brought the sport into disrepute through outbursts of bad temper. Up to now he has got away with such lapses through feeble FIA findings. Maybe appropriate penalties will be enforced for future misdemeanours. *David Coulthard* in a Scottish way, will confirm he possesses star quality as befits a true child, shrewd and persuasive, of his race. *Eddie Irvine*, typical Ulsterman, cavalier driving style, no respector of divas, often guilty of taking needless risks, has become more mature. Whether it will add up to racing greatness remains to be seen. *Jean Alesi* is an odd mixture. Off the track radiates Italian charm, but in a race becomes a different fellow. Jekyll and Hyde of the circuits. Wildness compensated by immense powers of recovery. *Damon Hill* has limited appeal. Not a dynamic personality, he makes a dull person seem interesting. Hopefully will be cured of a tendency to whinge. *Ralf Schumacher* has immense belief in himself, though enthusiasm and skill are often imperfectly wedded, at times scarcely more than nodding acquaintances. The challenge of a new team could be a tonic. Not so with *Rubens Barrichello,* who has given yeoman service to Stewart in an unreliable car, but with rare moments of brilliance.

Giancarlo Fisichella may revive the flagging fortunes of Benetton. Much depends on the new engine which was unveiled on a minor note. Fisichella was accepted as the best *jeune* in Formula One. No longer a rookie, the time has come to confirm that early promise. *Jacques Villeneuve* can be a meteoric driver but lacks the charismatic appeal of his father, Gilles – somewhat similar contrast between Damon and Graham Hill. Having a famous father can mean uncomplimentary comparisons. His last season with Williams did little for his confidence. *Mika Hakkinen* is another to lack charisma, yet the uncommunicative image is misleading. Language difficulties make him seem tongue-tied. He is the most reclusive personality on the circuit: in that sense the least known, but in 1998 he was magnificent, cool under pressure to become the second Finn, after Keke Rosberg in 1982, to win the world title. He could well repeat the feat.

The crystal ball predicts the obvious that the main contenders will again be McLaren and Ferrari. Jordan could be the dark horse if reliability is constant. Damon may be No. 1, but Heinz-Harald is no slouch and younger. Williams, after a frustrating season with no wins, are hopeful that the FW21 will be the answer. Alessandro Zanardi holds the key. Frank is a shrewd judge. Five constructor's titles in six seasons speaks for itself. He feels Zanardi is the man.

BAR's debut began on a controversial note by defying FIA ruling over livery. They announced that one car would be in the colours of Lucky Strike cigarette brand, the second to run with the 555 logo. Benetton, Prost and Sauber fancy their chances in the Millennium along with Minardi and even Arrows, whilst anything could happen with Stewart. It always occurs at the start of every season. Rose-tinted spectacles convince every team that the pre-race bally-hoo at launch parties is reality. Motor-racing magazines, short of news, pamper the illusion to fill pages in the off-season. Mistaking appetite for ability will always be with us.

An interesting item of news that may shape the political future of the sport after the century ends was the admission by Bernie Ecclestone that after all he is not immortal. He has named his heirs. The burden will be shared by three men, who will head the board of a public company to be floated on the stock-market provided the proposal survives an investigation by the European Union. If successful, this trio would be in charge of commercial ventures, in short, virtually all motor-racing activities. Such has been the reconstruction of the sport in which, apart from a brief interlude on television screens interrupted by adverts on Sunday afternoons, everything is dominated by the cash-nexus. The background of these gentlemen is significant. Marco Piccinini was a former Ferrari team manager. Walter Thoma used to head Philip Morris, owners of Marlboro. Helmut Werner made his mark as member of the Daimler-Benz board. Their combined influence will mould the sport. Many people feel uneasy at such an oligarchic approach. On a personal note, I hope this announcement does not mean Bernie's health is failing. Seeing him in action suggests the opposite. We may have differing views, but he is always good company. Nothing will change. He just gets worse. Some time ago we had a meal in the Dorchester Hotel in London. Suddenly, for no apparent reason, he asked what I thought of the Hyde Park Hotel. Not knowing it well, I replied that obviously it is first-class with an international reputation, why the question? "I was thinking of buying it." I could think of no suitable comment. Instead I offered another cup of coffee. And of course he could have bought it!

Maybe the decision to stand down indicates Bernie has contracted a variation of the Millennium bug.

Pause for a Moment

This list of names, by no means definitive, should be read with retrospective appreciation. In varying degrees, each man contributed to the lore of motor-racing. Most were close friends. Many died pursuing a sport that was their life. They mirror an attitude that belongs to another era. This is where the camera lens is invaluable. The camera freezes their images exactly as they were, reminders of the years when motor-racing was not dominated by the cash-nexus.

Bob Anderson
Alberto Ascari
Lorenzo Bandini
Vic Barlow
Count Goden de
  Beaufort
Jean Behra
Peter Berthon
Lucien Bianchi
John Bolster
Joakim Bonnier
Maxwell Boyd
Tony Brise

Chris Bristow
Sir David Brown
Ivor Bueb
Lord Camden
Rudolf Caracciola
Basil Cardew
François Cevert
Colin Chapman
Louis Chiron
Jim Clark
Peter Collins
Piers Courage
Mark Donohue

René Dreyfus
Courtenay Edwards
Giuseppe Farina
Enzo Ferrari
Ron Flockhart
Olivier Gendebien
Gregor Grant
Masten Gregory
Mike Hailwood
Eddie Hall
Paul Hawkins
Mike Hawthorn
Graham Hill

Denny Hulme
James Hunt
Earl Howe
Innes Ireland
Dick Jeffrey
Denis Jenkinson
Chris Lambert
Stuart Lewis-Evans
Willy Mairesse
Raymond Mays
Bruce McLaren
Harry Mundy
Luigi Musso

Gunnar Nilsson
Sir Alfred Owen
Carlos Pace
Ricardo Paletti
Mike Parkes
Reg Parnell
Ronnie Peterson
Dennis Poore
Marques Alfonso de
  Portago
Tom Pryce
Ian Raby
Lance Reventlow

Jochen Rindt
Pedro Rodriguez
Ricardo Rodriguez
Giacomo Russo
Lodovico Scarfiotti
Harry Schell
Jo Schlesser
Archie Scott-Brown
Wolfgang Seidel
Ayrton Senna
Jo Siffert
Moises Solana
Mike Spence

Alan Stacey
Hans Stuck
Piero Taruffi
Tony Vandervell
Gilles Villeneuve
Amherst Villiers
Prince Paul von
  Metternich
Count Wolfgang von
  Trips
Roger Williamson
Tom Wisdom
John Wyer

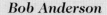

Bob Anderson

Ritchie Ginther

Jochen Rindt

Gerhard Mitter

Chris Irwin

Peter Berthon

Lorenzo Bandini

Bruce McLaren

Jim Clark

Graham Hill

Jean Behra

Juan Manuel Fangio

Ron Flockhart

Willy Mairesse

Masten Gregory

Ludovico Scarfiotti

Colin Chapman

Mike Parkes

Mike Spence

Luigi Scarlatti

David Brown

Index